THE LION
GRAPHIC

BIBLE

Illustrations by Jeff Anderson
Script by Mike Maddox
Lettering by Steve Harrison

A LION BOOK

Contents

THE OLD TESTAMENT

THE NEW TESTAMENT

This edition copyright © 2004 Lion Hudson
Text copyright © 1998 Mike Maddox
Illustrations copyright © 1998 Jeff Anderson
Lettering copyright © 1998 Steve Harrison

The moral rights of the author, illustrator
and letterer have been asserted

A Lion Book, an imprint of
Lion Hudson plc
Mayfield House, 256 Banbury Road,
Oxford OX2 7DH, England
www.lionhudson.com
ISBN 0 7459 4923 1

First hardback edition 1998
First paperback edition 2001
This edition 2004
10 9 8 7 6 5 4 3 2 1 0

All rights reserved

A catalogue record for this book is available
from the British Library

Printed and bound in Singapore

IN THE BEGINNING, GOD CREATED
THE HEAVENS AND THE EARTH.

THEN GOD SAID, 'LET THE LAND PRODUCE PLANT LIFE: GRASSES, HERBS, SEED-BEARING PLANTS, FRUIT-BEARING TREES, PLANTS OF EVERY KIND.' AND GOD SAW THAT IT WAS GOOD.

THERE WAS EVENING AND MORNING, AND THAT WAS THE THIRD DAY.

AND GOD SAID, 'LET THERE BE LIGHTS IN THE SKY TO SEPARATE DAY FROM NIGHT, AND TO SERVE AS SIGNS MARKING THE SEASONS, DAYS AND YEARS.'

SO GOD MADE TWO GREAT LIGHTS, ONE TO SHINE BY DAY, AND ONE TO SHINE BY NIGHT.

HE ALSO MADE THE STARS.

AND GOD SAW THAT IT WAS GOOD. THERE WAS EVENING AND MORNING, AND THAT WAS THE FOURTH DAY.

AND GOD SAID, 'LET THE OCEANS TEEM WITH LIFE, AND LET BIRDS FLY IN THE SKIES.'

SO GOD CREATED THE GREAT SEA CREATURES, AND EVERY LIVING THING IN THE OCEAN.

AND GOD WAS PLEASED WITH WHAT HE SAW, AND SAW THAT IT WAS GOOD.

GOD BLESSED THEM AND SAID, 'BE FRUITFUL AND INCREASE TO FILL THE SEAS AND SKIES.' THERE WAS EVENING AND MORNING, AND THAT WAS THE FIFTH DAY.

WHEN GOD MADE THE EARTH, HE MADE A MAN – 'ADAM' – FROM THE DUST OF THE DRY GROUND, BREATHING LIFE INTO HIM.

GOD PLANTED A GARDEN IN EDEN, AND THERE HE PUT THE MAN HE HAD CREATED. THE GARDEN WAS FULL OF BEAUTIFUL TREES THAT BORE DELICIOUS FRUIT.

IN THE MIDDLE OF THE GARDEN GOD SET THE TREE OF LIFE AND THE TREE OF THE KNOWLEDGE OF GOOD AND EVIL.

GOD GAVE ADAM CHARGE OF THE GARDEN, TO TAKE CARE OF IT AND TEND IT, SAYING; 'YOU ARE FREE TO EAT FROM ANY TREE IN THE GARDEN, EXCEPT THE TREE OF THE KNOWLEDGE OF GOOD AND EVIL.'

'IF YOU EAT ITS FRUIT, YOU ARE SURELY DOOMED TO DIE.'

GOD BROUGHT ALL THE BIRDS AND ANIMALS TO ADAM TO GIVE THEM THEIR NAMES.

THEN GOD SAID, 'IT'S NOT GOOD FOR ADAM TO BE ALONE. HE NEEDS A FITTING PARTNER TOO.'

SO GOD PUT ADAM INTO A DEEP SLEEP, AND WHILE HE WAS SLEEPING TOOK A RIB FROM HIS SIDE.

WITH THE RIB GOD MADE A WOMAN.

WHEN HE WOKE AND SAW WHAT GOD HAD DONE, ADAM SAID:

AT LAST! ONE OF MY OWN KIND.

BONE TAKEN FROM MY BONE, FLESH FROM MY FLESH, I WILL CALL YOU 'WOMAN' BECAUSE YOU WERE TAKEN OUT OF MAN.

THE MAN AND WOMAN WERE BOTH NAKED, BUT HAD NO FEELING OF SHAME.

A RIVER FLOWED FROM EDEN TO WATER THE GARDEN.
FROM THERE IT BRANCHED INTO FOUR STREAMS.

THE MAN AND THE WOMAN CULTIVATED THE GARDEN,
AND CARED FOR ALL THE ANIMALS.

IN THE CENTRE OF THE GARDEN WERE
THE TWO SPECIAL TREES GOD HAD PLANTED.
THE FIRST WAS CALLED THE TREE OF LIFE.

THE SECOND WAS THE TREE GOD HAD WARNED
THEM OF — THE TREE WHOSE FRUIT WOULD
CAUSE THEIR DEATHS IF THEY ATE IT.

THIS WAS THE TREE OF KNOWLEDGE — KNOWLEDGE NOT ONLY OF WHAT WAS GOOD —

BUT ALSO OF EVIL...

SO GOD BANISHED THE MAN AND THE WOMAN FROM HIS PRESENCE IN THE GARDEN. FOR LIGHT AND GOODNESS CANNOT COEXIST WITH DARKNESS AND EVIL.

AN ANGEL WITH A FLAMING SWORD WAS SET TO GUARD THE ENTRANCE, BARRING THE WAY TO THE TREE OF LIFE FOR EVER.

THEN ADAM NAMED HIS WIFE 'EVE', WHICH MEANS 'LIVING', BECAUSE SHE WOULD BE THE MOTHER OF THE HUMAN RACE.

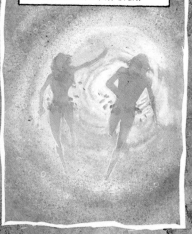

BEFORE THEY LEFT, GOD MADE GARMENTS OF ANIMAL SKIN FOR ADAM AND EVE TO WEAR.

THEIR LIFE FROM NOW ON WOULD BE EXACTLY AS GOD SAID: A STRUGGLE TO SURVIVE IN A WORLD TURNED HOSTILE AND DANGEROUS.

THEY WOULD KNOW TOIL AND PAIN UNTIL THE DAY THEY DIED AND THEY RETURNED TO THE DUST THEY WERE MADE FROM.

THE WORLD THEY KNEW NOW WAS A HARD, COLD PLACE COMPARED WITH THE BEAUTY OF EDEN.

ADAM AND EVE SLEPT TOGETHER. EVE BECAME PREGNANT AND GAVE BIRTH TO A SON, CALLED CAIN.

LATER SHE HAD ANOTHER SON, ABEL.

CAIN GREW UP TO WORK THE SOIL; ABEL BECAME A SHEPHERD.

IN TIME, CAIN BROUGHT SOME OF HIS HARVEST AS AN OFFERING TO GOD. ABEL BROUGHT THE BEST LAMB OF HIS FLOCK.

GOD WAS PLEASED WITH ABEL'S OFFERING, BUT NOT WITH CAIN'S. ABEL WAS A GOOD MAN, A MAN OF FAITH, BUT GOD COULD SEE THE DARKNESS IN CAIN'S HEART.

AND SO GOD SAID:

BUT CAIN REFUSED TO LISTEN TO GOD. HE BURNED WITH RAGE.

CAIN WAS FURIOUS.

WHY SO ANGRY, CAIN? NO NEED TO SCOWL IF YOU HAVE DONE RIGHT.

IF NOT, SIN IS CROUCHING BY THE DOOR OF YOUR LIFE. IT WANTS TO CONTROL YOU.

BUT YOU MUST FIGHT IT!

ALLOWING HIS ANGER TO RULE HIM, HE PLOTTED AGAINST HIS BROTHER...

17

EVERYONE IN THE BOAT BEFORE OLD NOAH GETS HIS BEARD WET!

QUICK, BEFORE IT STARTS RAINING FISH!

FOR THE LAST TIME, LEAVE US ALONE!

IS THAT FIGHTING TALK? I DO HOPE SO. IT WOULD BE MORE... ENTERTAINING IF YOU WOULD FIGHT INSTEAD OF BUILDING FLOATING FARMYARDS.

BAH! HIS GOD'S WARPED HIS BRAIN. IF HE TOLD HIM TO BALANCE GOATS ON HIS NOSE HE'D DO IT.

EITHER THAT OR TIE PADDLES TO THEIR LEGS!

BUT NOAH DID AS GOD HAD TOLD HIM.

450 FEET LONG, 75 FEET WIDE AND THREE STOREYS HIGH, THE BOAT WAS EVENTUALLY FINISHED.

WATERPROOF AND WITH A LOADING RAMP TO TAKE THE HEAVIEST LIVING CREATURES, IT HAD NO KEEL, NO SAILS NOR RUDDER — THIS WASN'T A SHIP BUILT FOR A VOYAGE OF DISCOVERY.

THIS WAS A LIFEBOAT.

BUT EVEN WITH THE BOAT COMPLETED, THE WORK WAS FAR FROM OVER FOR NOAH AND HIS FAMILY.

THE GATHERING AND STOCKING OF PROVISIONS FOR A LONG STAY WAS A TASK IN ITSELF. ESPECIALLY CONSIDERING THE NEEDS OF THEIR CARGO —

A BREEDING PAIR OF EVERY ANIMAL IN CREATION, ALL TO BE TAKEN INTO THE BOAT, CARED FOR AND FED — EACH WITH ITS OWN DIET AND NEEDS.

ALL OF THEM — TWO BY TWO.

THEY CALLED THE BOAT 'THE ARK', MEANING 'CHEST' OR 'BOX', FOR IT CONTAINED THE FUTURE OF ALL LIFE ON EARTH.

AND THE ANIMALS WOULD BREED AGAIN.

THIS WAS GOD'S PLAN, NOT NOAH'S. GOD KNEW THEIR NEEDS AND HOW BEST TO CARE FOR THEM.

AFTER ALL, THEY WERE THE WORK OF THE SAME CREATOR.

NOAH, AND THOSE WITH HIM IN THE ... WERE SPARED. NOAH HAD THREE ... THEY AND THEIR FAMILIES WOULD ...NUE THE HUMAN RACE.

...AINS FELL LIKE NO RAIN BEFORE OR SINCE, ...OWING CITIES, TOWNS AND MOUNTAINS.

FOR FORTY DAYS —

AND FORTY NIGHTS.

AND THEN, ALMOST AS SUDDENLY AS IT BEGAN —

IT STOPPED.

ABOUT TIME TOO!

IT'S OVER! HAVE ONE OF THE BOYS BRING A RAVEN UP FROM THE CARRION BIRDS SECTION — LET'S SEE IF THE WATERS ARE SHRINKING YET.

THE RAVEN FLEW AROUND THE ARK, BUT IT DID NOT STRAY FAR — MEANING THAT LAND HAD NOT YET APPEARED.

IN ITS BEAK IT CARRIED A FRESH OLI
BRANCH, THE FIRST GREENERY THE
CREW HAD SEEN SINCE THEIR VOYAGE
BEGAN. THE WATERS HAD BEGUN TO REI

IT WAS LATE IN THE
EVENING WHEN
IT RETURNED.

HE WAITED, AND THEN
SENT THE BIRD OUT AGAIN.

THEN NOAH RELEASED A DOVE.
AT FIRST IT RETURNED AS THERE
WAS NOWHERE FOR IT TO REST.

THEIR TIME TOGETHER ON
THE ARK WAS ALMOST OVER.

FREE AT LAST THE ANIMALS EXPLODED OUTWARDS
IN A DAZZLING BLAZE OF FUR AND FEATHERS. ALL
SHAPES AND SIZES, COLOURS AND SOUNDS, THEY
SPREAD TO THE FAR CORNERS OF THE WORLD.

NOAH AND HIS FAMILY WORSHIPPED
THEIR GOD ON THAT DAY, AND GOD
ANSWERED THEM, SAYING:

NEVER AGAIN
WILL I CURSE THE EARTH
BECAUSE OF WHAT PEOPLE
HAVE DONE. AS LONG AS THE
WORLD LASTS, THERE WILL BE SPRING
AND HARVEST, NIGHT AND DAY,
SUMMER AND WINTER,
DAY AND NIGHT.

GO: HAVE
MANY CHILDREN,
AND ALL THE WORLD WILL
BE YOURS.

THEN GOD AND NOAH MADE AN
AGREEMENT, A FORMAL COVENANT.

NEVER AGAIN WOULD GOD SEND A FLOOD TO
DESTROY THE EARTH, AND AS A SIGN HE SET
THE RAINBOW IN THE SKY SO THAT ALL LIVING
CREATURES COULD SEE GOD'S PROMISE.

NOAH'S SONS AND FAMILIES MOVED OUT INTO
THE WORLD WITH GOD'S BLESSING, AND AS
THEY MULTIPLIED THEY BUILT CITIES.

IT'S ONE THING FOR GOD TO TELL YOU WE'RE GOING TO HAVE A CHILD, BUT IT'S ANOTHER ACTUALLY HAVING IT. THE ONLY REASON I CAN THINK OF WHY WE HAVEN'T CHILDREN IS BECAUSE GOD IS STOPPING ME FROM HAVING THEM!

SO WHAT DO YOU SUGGEST?

HAGAR.

AND SO ABRAHAM DID WHAT SARAH SAID. HE SLEPT WITH HAGAR, HER SERVANT.

IT WAS SARAH'S IDEA, AFTER ALL.

HAGAR BECAME PREGNANT ALMOST AT ONCE, AND BEGAN TO FEEL SOMEHOW SUPERIOR TO HER MISTRESS, FUELLING POOR SARAH'S FEELINGS OF INADEQUACY.

FRUSTRATED AND JEALOUS, SHE TOOK HER ANGER OUT ON HAGAR, TREATING HER CRUELLY.

BY TAKING MATTERS INTO THEIR OWN HANDS, ABRAHAM AND SARAH HAD INTERFERED WITH GOD'S PLAN.

PREGNANT AND DESPERATELY UNHAPPY, HAGAR RAN AWAY ALONE, OUT INTO THE DESERT.

IT WAS TIME FOR GOD TO INTERVENE...

THE ANGEL OF THE LORD MET HAGAR OUT IN THE DESERT.

HAGAR! THE LORD KNOWS HOW UNHAPPY YOU ARE.

GO BACK TO SARAH. YOU WILL CALL YOUR CHILD 'ISHMAEL': THROUGH HIM YOU WILL HAVE TOO MANY DESCENDANTS TO COUNT. GOD KNOWS. HE CARES. GO BACK.

SO HAGAR RETURNED, TO GIVE BIRTH TO ISHMAEL. AT LAST ABRAHAM HAD A SON OF HIS OWN. COULD THIS HAVE BEEN WHAT GOD MEANT?

ABRAHAM WAS EIGHTY-SIX WHEN ISHMAEL WAS BORN. THE PAIN WAS ALMOST TOO MUCH FOR SARAH TO BEAR.

ISAAC WAS THE ANSWER TO YEARS OF PAINFUL LONGING.

HE WAS THEIR JOY, THEIR LOVE, THEIR FAITH IN GOD REALIZED, AND ALL THEIR DREAMS COME TRUE.

HE WAS ALMOST LIFE ITSELF TO THEM.

GOD WANTED ABRAHAM TO BE THE FATHER OF A PEOPLE THROUGH WHOM THE WORLD WOULD BE BLESSED. BUT FIRST THERE WOULD BE ONE MORE TEST...

AND SO ONE DAY ABRAHAM RECEIVED A MESSAGE FROM GOD. IT WAS THE MOST APPALLING NEWS.

WITH A HEAVY HEART ABRAHAM OBEYED THE MESSAGE, AND SET OFF WITH HIS YOUNG SON.

HE WAS TO TAKE THE BOY TO THE TOP OF A MOUNTAIN, AND SACRIFICE HIM AS A BURNT OFFERING TO GOD.

ABRAHAM HAD WANTED THIS SON SO BADLY, IT WAS AGONY TO LOSE HIM IN SUCH A HORRIFYING WAY.

ISAAC KNEW NOTHING OF ALL THIS. TO HIM THE DAY WAS A GREAT ADVENTURE WITH HIS FATHER.

SEE, FATHER? ALL THAT WOOD I CARRIED WILL BURN WELL! ALL WE NEED NOW IS A LAMB.

ISAAC WAS OUT IN THE FIELDS EARLY ONE EVENING, WHEN HE SAW CAMELS IN THE DISTANCE. THEY WERE HEADING DIRECTLY FOR HIS CAMP.

REBEKAH SAW ISAAC FROM AFAR, A LONE FIGURE, WALKING TOWARDS THEM THROUGH THE FIELDS.

ISAAC BROUGHT REBEKAH TO THE TENT OF HIS MOTHER, SARAH, AND THERE HE MARRIED HER.

THE PAIN HE FELT AT HIS MOTHER'S DEATH WAS REPLACED BY HIS LOVE FOR REBEKAH.

GOD HAD NOT ONLY FOUND HIM A WIFE, BUT HEALED HIS BROKEN HEART.

IN TIME, REBEKAH GAVE BIRTH TO TWINS, ALTHOUGH THEY WERE AS UNLIKE AS TWO BROTHERS COULD BE.

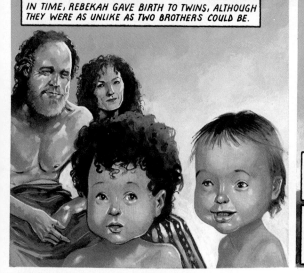

ESAU WAS THE ELDER. WHEN HE WAS BORN, HIS WHOLE BODY WAS COVERED IN HAIR, ALMOST AS IF HE WERE WEARING ROUGH CLOTHES.

HE BECAME A GREAT HUNTER, A MAN WHO LOVED THE HILLS, FIELDS, AND THE OPEN SKIES. ISAAC, WHO HAD A TASTE FOR WILD GAME, LOVED HIS SON GREATLY.

THE YOUNGER TWIN, JACOB, WAS THE EXACT OPPOSITE. A QUIET MAN WHO ENJOYED THE COMPANY OF OTHERS, HE WAS HIS MOTHER'S FAVOURITE.

GOD HAD TOLD ISAAC THAT THE TWO BOYS WOULD BE THE FATHERS OF TWO NATIONS, AND THAT THE FIRSTBORN WOULD BE SUBJECT TO THE OTHER.

ESAU LIVED ONLY FOR THE MOMENT. A FACT WHICH COST HIM DEAR AS HE GREW OLDER —

WHATEVER IS IT THAT YOU'RE COOKING, JACOB? IT SMELLS WONDERFUL. GIVE ME SOME BEFORE I STARVE TO DEATH!

YOU CAN SMELL FOOD A MILE AWAY.

ONLY WHEN I'M HUNGRY.

LIKE NOW FOR INSTANCE. COME ON, BEFORE IT GOES COLD!

BUT I'VE SPENT ALL DAY MAKING THIS. I KNOW IT'S YOUR FAVOURITE FOOD BUT I CAN'T JUST GIVE IT AWAY.

CAN I?

RED STEW, DONE JUST THE WAY YOU LIKE IT AND - OH! IS THAT THUNDER I CAN HEAR?

NO - IT'S YOUR STOMACH RUMBLING, MY MISTAKE.

I'LL TELL YOU WHAT, GIVE ME YOUR BIRTHRIGHT AND WE'LL CALL IT QUITS.

... MY BIRTHRIGHT?

MY, THAT DOES SMELL GOOD!

YES, YOUR BIRTHRIGHT. I MEAN, IT'S NOT AS IF YOU CAN EAT YOUR BIRTHRIGHT, IS IT? IT'S NOT AS IF YOUR BIRTHRIGHT WAS HERE IN FRONT OF YOU, DONE TO PERFECTION.

GOING COLD.

ALL RIGHT, ALL RIGHT! YOU CAN HAVE MY BIRTHRIGHT, JUST GIVE ME SOME STEW!

CERTAINLY. WOULD YOU LIKE SOME BREAD TOO?

HMMPH.

JACOB'S ACTIONS WERE RUTHLESS.

BUT ESAU, IN CARING MORE ABOUT HIS STOMA THAN HIS RIGHTS AS FIRSTBORN SON, HAD BEHAVED AS IF HIS FAMILY MEANT NO MORE TO HIM THAN A BOWL OF STEW.

JACOB NOW BELIEVED HE HAD A LEGITIMATE CLAIM TO ESAU'S INHERITANCE. THE FIRSTBORN SON WOULD HAVE A GREATER SHARE OF THE WILL, AND THIS WAS NOW JACOB'S.

BUT HIS SCHEMING WAS FAR FROM OVE

REBEKAH HAD MADE JACOB A SUIT OF GOATSKIN. TO A BLIND, DEAF OLD MAN, HE MIGHT JUST PASS AS ESAU.

QUICK? YES, ERM... GOD HELPED ME. HERE, EAT THIS STEW. I CAUGHT THE GAME MYSELF LIKE YOU SAID, SO THAT YOU'D GIVE ME YOUR BLESSING.

HMM. COME CLOSER, ERM...ESAU. LET ME TOUCH YOU.

YOU FEEL LIKE HIM, EVEN IF YOUR VOICE IS JACOB'S. ARE YOU REALLY MY SON ESAU?

I AM.

THEN YOU HAVE MY BLESSING.

MAY GOD GIVE YOU HEAVEN'S DEW, AND PLENTY OF GRAIN AND NEW WINE. MAY NATIONS SERVE YOU AND BOW DOWN BEFORE YOU.

RULE OVER EVERY MEMBER OF THIS FAMILY FOR EVER. MAY THOSE WHO CURSE YOU BE CURSED, AND THOSE WHO BLESS YOU BE BLESSED.

WELL, THAT WASN'T TOO HARD, WAS IT?

GOD HAD TOLD ISAAC THAT HIS FIRSTBORN SON WOULD BE SUBJECT TO THE YOUNGER TWIN. YET ISAAC GAVE ESAU THE BIRTHRIGHT ANYWAY. AND REBEKAH DECEIVED HER HUSBAND.

JACOB HAD HIS FULL INHERITANCE, BUT LIED AND CHEATED TO WIN WHAT HE SAW AS HIS BY RIGHT.

A FACT WHICH WOULD NOT ESCAPE ESAU WHEN HE RETURNED FROM HUNTING...

WAKE UP FATHER. IT'S ME, ESAU. SIT UP AND EAT THIS, THEN YOU CAN GIVE ME YOUR BLESSING.

WHAT DO YOU MEAN? YOU HAVEN'T ALREADY GIVEN ME THE BLESSING. I'VE ONLY JUST GOT HERE!

AFTER THE FIRST CONFUSION, ISAAC AND ESAU SOON PUT TWO AND TWO TOGETHER. BUT IT WAS TOO LATE – ISAAC HAD FORMALLY GIVEN THE FULL INHERITANCE TO JACOB.

JACOB! I'LL KILL HIM!

AND SO ESAU MADE PLANS. ISAAC WOULDN'T LIVE FOR EVER AND SO, AFTER A RESPECTABLE PERIOD OF MOURNING, ESAU WOULD MURDER HIS BROTHER.

JACOB HAD RECEIVED THE BIRTHRIGHT AS GOD INTENDED, BUT THE WHOLE FAMILY HAD LIED AND DECEIVED EACH OTHER IN THE PROCESS.

JACOB, THE QUIET HOME-LOVER, RAN AWAY INTO EXILE THROUGH FEAR OF HIS BROTHER. LEAVING THE CAMPS HE HAD LIVED IN ALL HIS LIFE, HE SET OUT FOR THE HOME OF HIS UNCLE LABAN, REBEKAH'S BROTHER.

HE NEVER SAW HIS BELOVED MOTHER AGAIN.

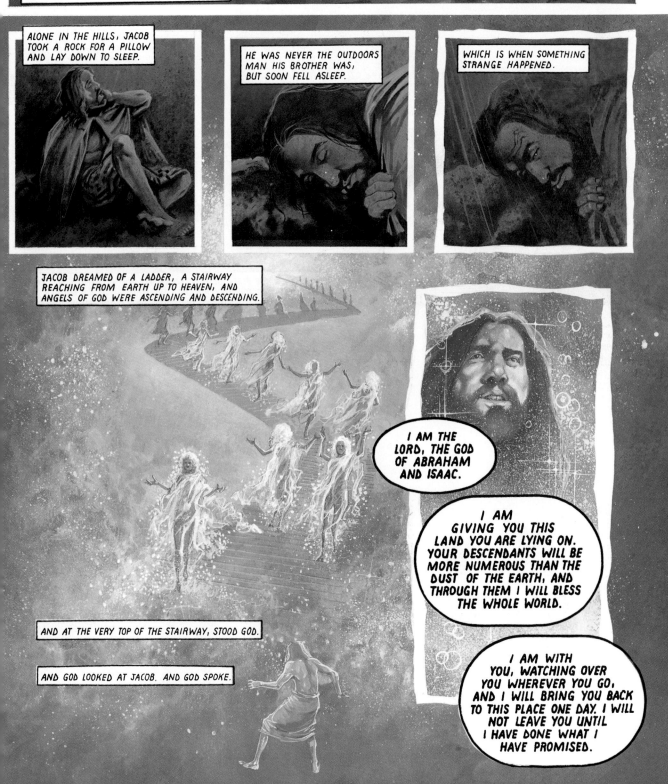

ALONE IN THE HILLS, JACOB TOOK A ROCK FOR A PILLOW AND LAY DOWN TO SLEEP.

HE WAS NEVER THE OUTDOORS MAN HIS BROTHER WAS, BUT SOON FELL ASLEEP.

WHICH IS WHEN SOMETHING STRANGE HAPPENED.

JACOB DREAMED OF A LADDER, A STAIRWAY REACHING FROM EARTH UP TO HEAVEN, AND ANGELS OF GOD WERE ASCENDING AND DESCENDING.

I AM THE LORD, THE GOD OF ABRAHAM AND ISAAC.

I AM GIVING YOU THIS LAND YOU ARE LYING ON. YOUR DESCENDANTS WILL BE MORE NUMEROUS THAN THE DUST OF THE EARTH, AND THROUGH THEM I WILL BLESS THE WHOLE WORLD.

AND AT THE VERY TOP OF THE STAIRWAY, STOOD GOD.

AND GOD LOOKED AT JACOB. AND GOD SPOKE.

I AM WITH YOU, WATCHING OVER YOU WHEREVER YOU GO, AND I WILL BRING YOU BACK TO THIS PLACE ONE DAY. I WILL NOT LEAVE YOU UNTIL I HAVE DONE WHAT I HAVE PROMISED.

JACOB WAS IN LOVE WITH RACHEL RIGHT FROM THE START. WHEN LABAN ASKED WHAT WAGES HE WOULD WANT FOR WORKING FOR HIM, JACOB OFFERED SEVEN YEARS' LABOUR IN RETURN FOR HER HAND IN MARRIAGE.

THIS WAS AN OFFER TOO GOOD FOR LABAN TO TURN DOWN.

AND SO JACOB SERVED SEVEN YEARS FOR RACHEL, BUT THE YEARS SEEMED NO MORE THAN DAYS, SO GREAT WAS HIS LOVE FOR HER.

HOWEVER... RACHEL HAD AN OLDER SISTER, NAMED LEAH, AND BY ALL ACCOUNTS SHE WASN'T QUITE THE BEAUTY RACHEL WAS.

FINDING A HUSBAND FOR RACHEL HAD BEEN EASY, AND LABAN HAD DONE VERY WELL OUT OF THE ARRANGEMENT, BUT THINGS WOULDN'T BE SO EASY ONCE JACOB'S SEVEN-YEAR CONTRACT WAS UP.

IF JACOB WAS A SCHEMER, HE'D MET HIS MATCH IN LABAN.

ANYWAY, THE SEVEN YEARS WERE UP, THE WEDDING BETWEEN RACHEL AND JACOB CAME AROUND, AND THERE WAS MUCH CELEBRATING AND FEASTING.

AND POSSIBLY DRINKING.

THE BRIDE LOOKED BEAUTIFUL IN HER WEDDING DRESS.

IN HER VEIL.

AT THE END OF THE EVENING, LABAN GAVE HIS DAUGHTER IN MARRIAGE TO JACOB AND WATCHED AS THEY WENT OFF TO BED.

IT WAS DARK.

SHE WORE A VEIL.

WHATEVER THE REASON, IT WASN'T UNTIL MORNING LIGHT THAT JACOB LOOKED AT HIS WIFE, AND SAID —

LEAH?! WHAT ARE YOU DOING HERE?!

I'M YOUR WIFE.

YOU MOST CERTAINLY ARE NOT!

I AM NOW.

LABAN! WHAT HAVE YOU DONE TO ME?! I WORK SEVEN YEARS FOR YOU, AND YOU MARRY ME TO THE WRONG DAUGHTER!

YOU MEAN LEAH? WHAT'S SO TERRIBLE ABOUT THAT?

WHEN JACOB FIRST CROSSED THE RIVER JORDAN, HE WAS RUNNING FROM HIS BROTHER, ESAU, AND OWNED NOTHING BUT THE STAFF HE LEANED ON. NOW, RETURNING HOME, HE HAD WIVES, CHILDREN, FLOCKS AND SERVANTS TO CARE FOR.

JACOB WAS SCARED OF TROUBLE AHEAD. EVERY STEP THEY TOOK TOWARDS CANAAN BROUGHT THEM CLOSER TO THE LANDS BELONGING TO ESAU.

ADVANCE SCOUTS AHEAD OF THEM REPORTED THAT ESAU HAD HEARD OF JACOB'S RETURN AND WAS RIDING TOWARDS THEM WITH 400 MEN.

THERE WAS UNFINISHED BUSINESS BETWEEN THE TWO BROTHERS, AND ESAU'S DEATH THREATS STILL HUNG HEAVY IN THE AIR.

JACOB FEARED THE WORST.

SPLITTING HIS PEOPLE INTO GROUPS, EACH LADEN WITH GIFTS FOR ESAU, HE SENT THEM ON AHEAD OF HIM. IN THIS WAY HE HOPED TO PACIFY HIS BROTHER, OR AT THE VERY LEAST GIVE THEM A BETTER CHANCE OF SURVIVAL SHOULD ESAU ATTACK.

HIS HERDS AND SERVANTS SENT ON, JACOB THEN SENT HIS WIVES, MAIDSERVANTS AND ALL ELEVEN SONS OVER THE RIVER.

AND SO HE WAS ALONE ONCE MORE.

JACOB HAD PRAYED TO THE GOD OF HIS FATHERS TO SAVE HIM FROM HIS BROTHER'S VENGEANCE.

THEN, AS NOW, JACOB HAD BEEN ALONE AND SCARED, TERRIFIED OF HIS BROTHER AND FEARING FOR HIS LIFE. BUT GOD HAD NOT FORGOTTEN JACOB, NOR THE PROMISES MADE ALL THOSE YEARS BEFORE.

AND NOW, AS BEFORE, GOD SPOKE TO JACOB...

A MAN CAME TO HIM IN THE NIGHT, AND THEY FOUGHT UNTIL DAYBREAK.

43

WHERE JACOB HAD EXPECTED VIOLENCE, ESAU HAD EMBRACED HIM AND WEPT WITH JOY AT HIS RETURN. HAPPY TO HAVE HIS BROTHER BACK ALIVE, ESAU SET OFF ONCE MORE.

WHY NOT COME WITH ME NOW?

I HAVE SHEEP AND COWS TO THINK OF, MANY OF THEM WITH YOUNG. WE'LL FOLLOW YOU AT OUR OWN PACE. ALL I WANT NOW IS FOR THINGS TO BE RIGHT BETWEEN US.

AND SO JACOB WAS HOME AT LAST.

HE BOUGHT FIELDS IN THE LAND OF CANAAN, AND THERE HE BUILT AN ALTAR TO THE GOD OF ISRAEL — **HIS** GOD.

RACHEL, JACOB'S BELOVED WIFE, DIED GIVING BIRTH TO A SECOND SON, CALLED BENJAMIN.

RACHEL WAS BURIED ON THE ROAD TO BETHLEHEM, AND OVER HER TOMB JACOB SET A PILLAR.

ALTHOUGH SAFE IN THE LAND OF CANAAN, JACOB'S FAMILY LIFE WAS NO MORE PEACEFUL THAN IT HAD BEEN BEFORE. SINCE HE HAD CHILDREN BY FOUR WOMEN, TWO OF WHOM WERE SISTERS, HOW COULD IT BE?

BENJAMIN WAS THE LAST OF JACOB'S CHILDREN.

GOD HAD GIVEN JACOB MANY SONS, YET JACOB WAS BLIND TO THEIR FEELINGS AND OPENLY FAVOURED JOSEPH ABOVE THE REST. HE HAD BEEN BORN TO HIM LATE IN LIFE, AND WAS RACHEL'S FIRST SON.

AS A SIGN OF AFFECTION, JACOB GAVE JOSEPH A COAT, RICHLY DECORATED WITH MANY COLOURS.

HIS BROTHERS BECAME INCREASINGLY WORRIED. DID THIS MEAN THAT JACOB INTENDED TO GIVE EVERYTHING TO JOSEPH, WHEN IT WAS THEY WHO HAD DONE ALL THE HARD WORK?

AS IF THIS WEREN'T BAD ENOUGH, JOSEPH STARTED HAVING STRANGE DREAMS...

THE STORY OF JOSEPH

46

HEY, JOSEPH! WE'VE SOME COMPANY FOR YOU!

BUT I'M *INNOCENT*! THERE'S BEEN A TERRIBLE *MISTAKE*!

THAT'S WHAT THEY *ALL* SAY! YOU'LL LIKE THESE TWO, JOSEPH! FORMER KING'S OFFICIALS, LIKE YOU!

WELL, WE'RE STUCK HERE TOGETHER, WE MAY AS WELL *TRY* TO GET ALONG.

WHAT'S THE POINT? I'M HAUNTED BY *DREAMS*. I CAN'T GET THEM OUT OF MY *HEAD*.

ME TOO. THE SAME DREAM EVERY NIGHT, AND THERE'S NO ONE HERE TO INTERPRET THEM FOR US.

INTERPRETATIONS BELONG TO *GOD*. IT WAS DREAMS THAT GOT ME IN TROUBLE IN THE FIRST PLACE; BUT SEEING AS WE'RE ALREADY *IN* TROUBLE, WHY DON'T YOU TELL ME ABOUT THEM?

I USED TO BE THE PHARAOH'S *CUPBEARER*, BEFORE I OFFENDED HIM. IN MY DREAM I SAW THREE GRAPEVINES. I SQUEEZED THE GRAPES INTO MY MASTER'S CUP, AND GAVE IT TO HIM. I DON'T KNOW WHAT IT MEANS, AND THE WORRY IS MAKING ME SICK.

I HAD A DREAM TOO. I WAS THE PHARAOH'S MASTER *BAKER*, BEFORE I OFFENDED HIM. I DREAMT I HAD THREE BREADBASKETS. ONE WAS FULL OF BREAD FOR THE PHARAOH, BUT BIRDS CAME AND ATE *EVERYTHING*.

THE THREE *GRAPEVINES* REPRESENT THREE *DAYS*. IN THREE DAYS' TIME THE PHARAOH WILL RESTORE YOU TO YOUR POSITION, AND YOU WILL CARRY HIS CUP AS BEFORE.

THE THREE BASKETS *ALSO* REPRESENT THREE DAYS. THREE DAYS FROM NOW THE PHARAOH WILL HAVE YOUR SENTENCE CHANGED FROM LIFE IMPRISONMENT TO *DEATH*.

THE THIRD DAY WAS THE PHARAOH'S BIRTHDAY, AND HE GAVE A GREAT FEAST FOR ALL HIS OFFICIALS. HE PARDONED THE CUPBEARER AND RESTORED HIM TO HIS FORMER OFFICE: BUT THE BAKER HE HAD *HANGED*.

UNTIL SOME YEARS LATER...

GOD HAD BEEN AT WORK IN EGYPT. WHILE JOSEPH WAS IN PRISON, EVENTS HAD TAKEN PLACE THAT WOULD NOT ONLY CHANGE JOSEPH'S FUTURE, BUT HIS PEOPLE'S, AND THROUGH THEM, THE *WORLD*...

THE CUPBEARER DIDN'T GIVE JOSEPH A SECOND THOUGHT...

JOSEPH! ON YOUR FEET, MAN, *QUICKLY*!

ARE YOU MY *EXECUTIONER*?

HARDLY. YOU'LL NEED A SHAVE AND A CLEAN CHANGE OF CLOTHES. WE'RE TAKING YOU TO SEE THE *PHARAOH*!

AND SO THE SON OF JACOB CAME FACE TO FACE WITH THE MOST POWERFUL MAN ON EARTH — THE **PHARAOH!**

MY CUPBEARER HAS CONFESSED THAT HE HAS DONE YOU A GREAT **DISSERVICE,** HEBREW. YOU SHOWED HIM A KINDNESS, AND YET HE SOON **FORGOT** YOU. HE HAS SINCE BEEN **REMINDED** OF HIS SHORTCOMINGS. I AM TOLD YOU CAN INTERPRET **DREAMS,** JOSEPH. IS THIS **TRUE** ?

NO, YOUR MAJESTY. IT IS **NOT.**

BUT GOD WILL GIVE PHARAOH THE ANSWER HE DESIRES.

YOUR **GOD** ? VERY WELL.

I DREAMT I STOOD ON THE BANKS OF THE RIVER **NILE,** WHEN SEVEN COWS, SLEEK AND FATTENED, EMERGED FROM THE WATERS TO GRAZE AMONG THE REEDS.

BUT THE SEVEN FAT COWS WERE PURSUED BY SEVEN THIN COWS. UGLY, WASTED AND ULCEROUS, THEY ATE THE SEVEN FATTENED COWS, BUT LOOKED NO BETTER FOR IT. THEY LOOKED AS **DISEASED** AS THEY HAD BEFORE.

I DREAMT OF SEVEN HEALTHY EARS OF CORN, WITHERED AND STRANGLED BY SEVEN BLIGHTED EARS OF CORN, SCORCHED BY THE WIND.

I AM TROUBLED, JOSEPH. I HAVE CONSULTED THE MAGICIANS AND WISE MEN, BUT THEY HAVE BEEN NO HELP TO ME. TELL ME, WHAT DOES THIS MEAN ?

52

AND SO IT WAS THAT IN THE SECOND YEAR OF THE GREAT FAMINE, JACOB TOOK HIS WHOLE HOUSEHOLD, AND SET OUT ON ONE LAST GREAT JOURNEY.

GOD APPEARED TO JACOB IN A DREAM ONE MORE TIME. 'DO NOT BE AFRAID OF GOING TO EGYPT,' GOD TOLD HIM. 'YOUR CHILDREN WILL BE A GREAT NATION, AND ONE DAY I SHALL LEAD YOUR PEOPLE BACK TO CANAAN.'

ALTHOUGH THE LAND HAD GIVEN UP ON LIFE, GOD STILL STUCK TO THE PROMISES HE HAD MADE TO JACOB.

IT WAS ALL TOO WONDERFUL FOR WORDS.

JOSEPH WAS NOT DEAD, BUT RULED OVER THE MOST POWERFUL NATION ON EARTH.

FATHER?

IS THAT YOU? IS IT *REALLY* YOU?

HERE, LET ME LOOK AT YOU. IT'S BEEN SO VERY LONG, AND YOU'VE CHANGED SO MUCH. I NEVER THOUGHT I'D SEE YOU AGAIN. I WAS SURE YOU MUST BE DEAD.

I LIVE, FATHER. IT'S REALLY ME.

I'M *JOSEPH.*

OH MY BOY! I AM READY TO DIE NOW THAT I'VE SEEN YOU WITH MY OWN EYES! THE GOD OF YOUR FATHER, THE GOD OF ISAAC AND ABRAHAM HAS SAVED US!

THE FAMINE RAVAGED THE LAND, AND THE SOIL REFUSED TO YIELD CROPS. ALL AROUND, HARVESTS FAILED, LIVESTOCK PERISHED AND PEOPLE STARVED.

AND YET EGYPT SURVIVED. AND BECAUSE JOSEPH SURVIVED HIS FAMILY DID TOO.

ALL THROUGH THE FAMINE YEARS THE CHILDREN OF JACOB, ALSO CALLED **ISRAEL**, LIVED ON IN EGYPT. THE TWELVE SONS OF ISRAEL WOULD BECOME TWELVE TRIBES, AND THEIR PEOPLE CALLED THE **ISRAELITES**, THE CHILDREN OF ISRAEL.

AS A YOUNG MAN JACOB HAD FLED HIS FAMILY IN TERROR, FLEEING FOR HIS LIFE WITH NO POSSESSIONS, FRIENDS NOR FUTURE.

YET NOW HE WAS THE FATHER OF PHAROAH'S RIGHT-HAND MAN.

WHEN JACOB DIED, HE WAS GIVEN A **KING'S** BURIAL.

HIS BODY WAS RETURNED TO CANAAN, WHERE IT WAS LAID BESIDE ABRAHAM AND SARAH, AND ISAAC AND REBEKAH.

JOSEPH HIMSELF LIVED TO BE VERY OLD. AND DESPITE HIS BROTHERS' FEARS, HE FORGAVE THEM COMPLETELY FOR THEIR EARLIER CRUELTY.

ALTHOUGH JOSEPH WAS BURIED IN EGYPT, HIS WILL INSTRUCTED THE ISRAELITES TO TAKE HIS BONES WITH THEM WHEN THEY FINALLY RETURNED HOME. HE WOULD BE LAID TO REST WITH HIS FORBEARS.

AND SO THE ISRAELITES GREW IN NUMBERS IN EGYPT. AND WHILE THE YEARS TURNED TO DECADES —

AND THE DECADES TO **CENTURIES** —

THE JOURNEYS WERE FAR FROM OVER FOR THE CHILDREN OF ISRAEL.

THEIR TROUBLES WERE ONLY **BEGINNING**.

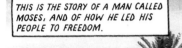

THE STORY OF MOSES

NEARLY 300 YEARS HAVE PASSED SINCE THE TIME OF JOSEPH AND THE GREAT FAMINE. DARK TIMES HAVE FALLEN ON EGYPT.

JACOB'S RACE, THE ISRAELITES, HAVE BECOME SLAVES TO THE EGYPTIANS. DESPITE THIS THEY STILL CLING TO LIFE, AND EVEN INCREASE IN NUMBERS.

THE NEW PHARAOH ORDERS A FINAL SOLUTION TO THE ISRAELITE 'PROBLEM' — ALL NEWBORN BABY BOYS ARE TO BE DROWNED AT BIRTH IN THE RIVER NILE.

THIS IS THE STORY OF A MAN CALLED MOSES, AND OF HOW HE LED HIS PEOPLE TO FREEDOM.

IN THE END SHE TOOK HIM TO THE NILE HERSELF.

BUT NOT TO BE DROWNED. PLACING HIM IN A BASKET WATERPROOFED WITH TAR, SHE PUSHED HIM OUT INTO THE REEDS.

BORN AT THE TIME OF THE PERSECUTION, THE BABY MOSES WAS KEPT UNDETECTED FOR THREE MONTHS. HIS MOTHER KNEW IT WAS ONLY A MATTER OF TIME BEFORE HE WAS DISCOVERED.

IT HAPPENED THAT ONE OF THE PHARAOH'S DAUGHTERS HAD GONE DOWN TO THE RIVER TO BATHE. IT WAS TOWARDS HER THAT THE LITTLE BASKET GENTLY FLOATED, TAKING WITH IT THE BABY INSIDE.

THE PHARAOH'S DAUGHTER HEARD THE BABY CRYING.

SHE HAD NO IDEA WHERE THE BABY HAD COME FROM. BUT WATCHING FROM CLOSE BY TO MAKE SURE THE BABY WAS SAFE WAS AN OLDER SISTER OF MOSES.

PHARAOH'S DAUGHTER DECIDED TO MAKE THE CHILD HER OWN. AND SO THE ABANDONED CHILD OF AN OPPRESSED SLAVE WAS TAKEN OUT OF DANGER, AND INTO THE VERY HEART OF PHARAOH'S PALACE.

MOSES GREW UP IN THE PHARAOH'S PALACE, SAFE FROM HARM IN THE HOUSE OF THE VERY MAN WHO WANTED TO EXTERMINATE HIS RACE.

IF HE'D ANY IDEA OF THE TROUBLE MOSES WOULD CAUSE EGYPT LATER, THE PHARAOH WOULD PROBABLY HAVE KILLED HIM WITH HIS OWN HANDS, THERE AND THEN.

YOUNG MOSES LIVED A PRIVILEGED LIFE IN THE ROYAL HOUSEHOLD, WHILE ALL AROUND HIM HIS FELLOW ISRAELITES SUFFERED AT THE HANDS OF THEIR MASTERS.

HE WATCHED AS HE GREW, WAITING FOR THE CHANCE TO STRIKE BACK.

ONE DAY HE SAW AN EGYPTIAN SAVAGELY BEATING AN ISRAELITE – AND SOMETHING INSIDE HIM SNAPPED...

PLEASE! NO MORE!

HE'S HAD ENOUGH! STOP IT!

DIDN'T YOU HEAR ME?

I SAID STOP!

WHO DO YOU THINK YOU ARE? HE'S MY SLAVE! AND ANYWAY HE'S ONLY AN ISRAELITE!

IT WAS ONLY AFTERWARDS THAT MOSES REALIZED WHAT HE HAD DONE...

MOSES HAD MADE SURE THERE WERE NO WITNESSES BEFORE CALLING TO THE MAN, AND THINKING NO ONE WAS LOOKING, HE STRUCK THE MAN DEAD.

SO MOSES LIVED THE LIFE OF A SHEPHERD, TENDING JETHRO'S HERDS. THE OLD LIFE OF LUXURY AND PRIVILEGE IN THE PALACE BEHIND HIM, MOSES ACQUIRED NEW SKILLS.

HE LEARNED HOW TO SURVIVE IN THE WILDERNESS; THINGS HE COULD NEVER HAVE KNOWN ABOUT IN THE COMFORT AND SAFETY OF THE PALACE.

...WHICH CAME AS A GREAT SURPRISE TO THE LAST MAN EVER TO EXPECT A PERSONAL CALL FROM GOD —

MOSES.

HE WAS TENDING THE SHEEP ON THE SLOPES OF MOUNT SINAI WHEN HE SAW A BUSH ON FIRE. AS HE WENT TO HAVE A CLOSER LOOK HE SAW THAT ALTHOUGH THE BRANCHES FLAMED, THE BUSH ITSELF WAS COMPLETELY UNHARMED.

ALL THE WHILE THE ISRAELITES REMAINED IN SLAVERY. THEIR CRIES FOR HELP WENT UP TO GOD, WHO HAD NOT FORGOTTEN THE PROMISES MADE TO ABRAHAM AND ISAAC AND JACOB. IT WAS TIME FOR GOD TO ACT IN MORE DIRECT WAYS.

MOSES!

IT WAS THEN THAT A VOICE SPOKE TO HIM.

WHO IS THERE?

MOSES WAS TERRIFIED.

I AM THE GOD OF ABRAHAM AND ISAAC AND JACOB.

TAKE YOUR SHOES OFF, FOR YOU ARE STANDING ON HOLY GROUND.

I HAVE SEEN THE MISERY OF MY PEOPLE IN EGYPT, AND I HAVE COME TO RESCUE THEM, TO TAKE THEM TO A LAND OVERFLOWING WITH MILK AND HONEY.

GO TO THE PHARAOH AND BRING THE ISRAELITES OUT OF EGYPT.

ME?

WHO'LL BELIEVE ME? I'M NOT A GOOD SPEAKER!

WHO MAKES MEN SPEAK? WHO MAKES THEM SEE AND HEAR? I DO. YOU HAVE A BROTHER, AARON; HE CAN SPEAK FOR YOU. I WILL HELP YOU BOTH.

PLEASE — SEND SOMEONE ELSE!

GO AND GATHER THE LEADERS OF ISRAEL TOGETHER. TELL THEM THAT THEIR GOD HAS SENT YOU TO LEAD THEM – THEY WILL BELIEVE YOU. THEN GO TO THE PHARAOH, AND I WILL MAKE HIM LET MY PEOPLE GO.

HOW WILL THEY BELIEVE ME?

YOU ARE HOLDING A STAFF. THROW IT TO THE GROUND AND THEN WATCH.

MOSES DID AS GOD SAID, AND THE STAFF TURNED INTO A SNAKE.

NOW — PICK IT UP BY THE TAIL.

AND MOSES PICKED UP THE SNAKE —

AND IT WAS A STAFF AGAIN.

SHOW THEM THIS, AND THEY WILL BELIEVE YOU. NOW GO — BRING MY PEOPLE OUT OF EGYPT.

AND SO MOSES WENT.

TAKING HIS WIFE AND SONS, HE LEFT JETHRO AND THE LIFE OF A SHEPHERD, AND RETURNED TO EGYPT.

THE LEADERS OF THE ISRAELITES WERE MORE THAN WILLING TO LISTEN TO MOSES, ESPECIALLY SINCE HIS BROTHER AARON DID MOST OF THE TALKING.

THE PLAN WAS SIMPLE: THE ISRAELITES WOULD ASK FOR THREE DAYS' RELEASE FROM WORK, TO GO TO THE DESERT AND WORSHIP THEIR GOD. ONCE ASSEMBLED, THEY WOULD MAKE A BREAK FOR FREEDOM.

CONVINCING PHARAOH WAS ANOTHER MATTER ALTOGETHER.

MY BROTHER AND I SPEAK FOR THE ENTIRE ISRAELITE PEOPLE. WE ASK PERMISSION TO CROSS THE BORDER FOR THREE DAYS TO WORSHIP OUR GOD — IN THE DESERT.

THREE DAYS. IS THAT ALL?

I DON'T THINK YOU'RE WORKING HARD ENOUGH AS IT IS, AND NOW YOU WANT THREE DAYS' HOLIDAY?

IS THIS WHAT YOU ARE TELLING ME, YOU POOR THINGS?

I THINK YOU'RE JUST LAZY.

HAVE THE OVERSEERS INCREASE THE WORKLOAD OF ALL ISRAELITES.

THE ISRAELITES WERE BEING WORKED HALF TO DEATH AS IT WAS. DESPITE THIS, THE PHARAOH'S ORDERS WERE ENFORCED.

BRUTALLY.

THE ISRAELITE FOREMEN SOON CAME TO RESENT MOSES' INTERFERENCE. PHARAOH NOW HAD EVEN MORE REASON TO HATE THEM. THE MORE THEY BEGGED FOR MERCY, THE HARDER PHARAOH WORKED THEM.

SO MOSES PRAYED ONCE MORE –

LORD GOD, WHY HAVE YOU CAUSED SO MUCH TROUBLE FOR US? SINCE I WENT TO SEE PHARAOH, THINGS HAVE ONLY GOT WORSE.

I AM THE LORD WHO SPOKE TO ABRAHAM, TO ISAAC AND JACOB. I MADE A PROMISE TO THEM, AND I HAVE NOT FORGOTTEN IT. GO BACK TO THE PHARAOH AND TELL HIM TO RELEASE MY PEOPLE.

BUT HE WON'T LISTEN TO ME!

TAKE AARON, YOUR BROTHER. HE WILL SPEAK FOR YOU AND PHARAOH WILL LISTEN. I WILL PUNISH THE EGYPTIANS FOR WHAT THEY HAVE DONE. THEY WILL RELEASE YOU.

AND SO MOSES WENT TO SEE THE PHARAOH. HE WOULD TELL HIM STRAIGHT: RELEASE THE ISRAELITES, OR UNIMAGINABLE PLAGUES AND DISASTERS WOULD RAVAGE HIS COUNTRY. GOD'S PLANS HAD TO BE FULFILLED. BUT THE PHARAOH JUST LAUGHED...

MOSES, YOU AMUSE ME! I HAVE MAGICIANS WHO CAN DO ALL THE THINGS YOU DESCRIBE, I'M NOT AFRAID OF CONJURING TRICKS!

COME AARON, WE'VE WARNED HIM. WE CAN DO NO MORE.

AND SO IT STARTED. TEN PLAGUES IN ALL CAME ON EGYPT, EACH WORSE THAN THE LAST. FIRST WAS THE PLAGUE OF BLOOD – THE RIVER NILE, LIFELINE OF THE EGYPTIAN PEOPLE, TURNED TO BLOOD.

THEN A PLAGUE OF FROGS, DRIVEN FROM THE FILTHY WATERS AND THE ROTTING FISH. THEY INVADED THE STREETS AND HOUSES, WHERE THEY DIED, ADDING TO THE STENCH.

THEN A PLAGUE OF GNATS, AND A PLAGUE OF FLIES, FEEDING ON THE ROTTING FISH AND FROGS.

BUT STILL PHARAOH REFUSED TO LET THE ISRAELITES GO.

THEN CAME A PLAGUE ON THE LIVESTOCK, FOLLOWED BY A PLAGUE OF BOILS AND SKIN INFECTIONS ON THE PEOPLE.

A PLAGUE OF HAILSTONES FELL, DESTROYING CROPS THE LENGTH OF THE COUNTRY. THEN A PLAGUE OF LOCUSTS, FINISHING OFF WHAT THE HAILSTONES HAD LEFT.

STILL PHARAOH REFUSED TO LET THE ISRAELITES GO.

THEN CAME A PLAGUE OF DARKNESS. NINE PLAGUES HAD FALLEN SO FAR, BUT ONE WAS STILL TO COME. AND IT WOULD BE THE WORST...

PHARAOH HAS BEEN GIVEN ONE FINAL CHANCE, BUT HE HAS REFUSED. HE TOLD ME TO GET OUT OF HIS SIGHT, AND I INTEND TO DO JUST THAT! ONE MORE PLAGUE WILL COME, AND THEN HE WILL RELEASE US. BUT WE MUST BE PREPARED.

TONIGHT IS A SPECIAL NIGHT. FROM NOW ON WE WILL MARK THIS AS THE FIRST DAY IN OUR CALENDAR, IT'S SO IMPORTANT.

EVERY ISRAELITE FAMILY MUST TAKE THEIR BEST LAMB, AND SLAUGHTER IT – IF THEY'RE TOO POOR, THEN SHARE WITH THEIR NEIGHBOUR. THEY MUST TAKE SOME BLOOD AND MAKE A MARK ON THEIR DOORFRAMES.

THEY MUST ROAST THE LAMB AND EAT IT WITH BREAD MADE WITHOUT YEAST. IT'S VITAL WE DO THIS TONIGHT, AND THROUGHOUT ALL GENERATIONS TO COME.

SOMETHING DREADFUL IS GOING TO HAPPEN TO EGYPT, BUT THOSE OF US WHO FOLLOW THESE INSTRUCTIONS WILL BE LEFT UNHARMED.

AT MIDNIGHT GOD STRUCK EGYPT. THE ELDEST CHILD OF EVERY EGYPTIAN, FROM THE PHARAOH ON HIS THRONE TO THE LOWEST PRISONER IN HIS DUNGEON, DIED.

THIS WAS THE PLAGUE OF THE FIRSTBORN, AND THE WORST OF ALL.

WAILING AND CRYING FILLED THE STREETS.

BUT DEATH PASSED OVER THE ISRAELITES.

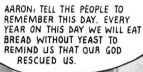

AT LAST PHARAOH LET THEM GO.

THE EGYPTIAN PEOPLE WERE SO KEEN TO SEE THE BACK OF THE ISRAELITES THAT THEY EVEN GAVE THEM GOLD AND SILVER, FOOD AND LIVESTOCK.

AARON, TELL THE PEOPLE TO REMEMBER THIS DAY. EVERY YEAR ON THIS DAY WE WILL EAT BREAD WITHOUT YEAST TO REMIND US THAT OUR GOD RESCUED US.

IT WILL BE A SIGN, AS PLAIN AS IF WE'D TIED A NOTE TO OUR FOREHEADS OR WRISTS.

THE FIRSTBORN OF ALL ISRAEL, EVEN THE LIVESTOCK, NOW BELONG TO GOD. WE ARE ALL UNDER HIS PROTECTION.

ALL ISRAEL LEFT EGYPT, EVEN JOSEPH'S BONES WERE CARRIED WITH THEM. AT LONG LAST HE COULD BE BROUGHT HOME FOR BURIAL. THE LONG JOURNEY HOME HAD BEGUN.

BACK IN EGYPT, THE NATION SLOWLY RECOVERED FROM THE RAVAGES OF THE PLAGUES, GIVING SOME PEOPLE TIME TO THINK CLEARLY AGAIN...

HE'S BEEN LIKE THIS FOR DAYS. HE'S NEVER BEEN SO QUIET.

IT WON'T LAST.

AFTER ALL THE TROUBLE THEY CAUSED, I SIMPLY LET THEM GO? HAVE I LOST MY MIND?

GUARDS! SUMMON THE CHARIOTEERS! CALL THE FASTEST MEN IN THE LAND! I WANT THE ISRAELITES BROUGHT BACK!

I WANT THEM BACK!

SO MOSES RAISED HIS STAFF OVER THE SEA AS GOD SAID.

AND AS HE DID SO A STRONG WIND CAME IN FROM THE EAST.

MOSES STOOD THERE ALL NIGHT, HIS STAFF OVER THE SEA, AND IN THE MORNING

THE WATERS

HAD PARTED.

I DON'T BELIEVE IT.

AND SO THEY PASSED UNHARMED ACROSS THE SEA. EVERY MAN, WOMAN AND CHILD, THEIR FLOCKS AND HERDS, AND WHAT POSSESSIONS THEY COULD CARRY.

ALL PASSED SAFELY ACROSS THE SEA.

WHO IS LIKE YOU, MY GOD?

THE NATIONS WILL HEAR OF THIS, AND OUR ENEMIES WILL MELT BEFORE US! YOUR UNFAILING LOVE WILL LEAD US, AND YOU WILL REIGN FOR EVER!

AFTER THEM! FOLLOW THEM ACROSS!

AFTER ALL, IF AN ARMY OF SLAVES COULD CROSS THE RED SEA UNHARMED, WHY SHOULDN'T THEY? IN THEIR CHARIOTS THEY WOULD BE ACROSS IN NO TIME AT ALL.

AND IF THEY WEREN'T HUNGRY, THEY WERE THIRSTY.

DID I CREATE THESE PEOPLE? DO I HAVE TO CARRY THEM IN MY ARMS THE WHOLE DISTANCE? NO. BUT IT FELT LIKE IT AT TIMES.

LORD GOD, WHAT AM I GOING TO DO WITH ALL THESE PEOPLE? IF I DON'T FIND THEM WATER SOON THEY'LL SURELY STONE ME TO DEATH!

MOSES, THERE'S NO WATER OUT HERE!

DID YOU BRING US HERE SO WE COULD DIE OF THIRST? DO YOU WANT TO KILL OUR CHILDREN? WE HOLD YOU RESPONSIBLE!

BUT GOD SPOKE TO ME, EVEN AS THE PEOPLE PICKED UP STONES TO KILL ME.

GOD TOLD ME TO GO WITH THE ELDERS, AND STRIKE THE ROCKS WITH MY STAFF. GOD WOULD STAND BEFORE ME, AND WATER WOULD COME OUT OF THE GROUND.

SO I TOOK MY STAFF, AND RAISED IT HIGH IN THE AIR —

CRACK! I BROUGHT IT DOWN ON THE ROCKS!

AND WATER CAME OUT.

THEN THERE WERE THE BATTLES. AFTER ALL, WE WEREN'T THE ONLY PEOPLE IN THE DESERT. THE AMALEKITES CAME AND ATTACKED US, BUT GOD WAS WITH US.

I SENT JOSHUA TO LEAD OUR FORCES, AND THEN WENT TO THE TOP OF THE HILL OVERLOOKING THE BATTLE.

IT WAS THEN I HAD A WELCOME VISITOR — JETHRO, MY FATHER-IN-LAW. HE HAD HEARD OF ALL THAT HAD HAPPENED SINCE WE LEFT EGYPT, AND CAME TO JOIN US, BRINGING ME SOME ADVICE...

MOSES, WHY DO YOU INSIST ON DOING EVERYTHING YOURSELF? THERE'S TOO MUCH WORK FOR ONE MAN. THERE ARE OTHERS WHO CAN HELP.

IT'S RIGHT TH... REPRESENT THE BEFORE GOD, AND THEM, AP... PEOPLE TO SORT O... MINOR ARGUM... FOR YO...

AS LONG AS I HELD MY STAFF IN THE AIR, WE TRIUMPHED. BUT IF I LOWERED MY ARMS, WE WOULD START TO LOSE. I BECAME SO TIRED THAT AARON AND HUR HAD TO HOLD MY ARMS UP FOR ME.

JOSHUA AND HIS MEN FOUGHT WELL, BUT IT WAS ONLY BECAUSE GOD WAS WITH US THAT WE WON.

"FIND GOD-FEARING MEN WHO CAN'T BE BRIBED, WHO CAN DECIDE WHICH CASES TRULY DESERVE YOUR ATTENTION, AND LET THEM SORT OUT THE REST THEMSELVES."

THREE MONTHS TO THE DAY AFTER LEAVING EGYPT, WE CAME TO THE SINAI DESERT AND CAMPED AT THE FOOT OF MOUNT SINAI ITSELF.

IT WAS ON MOUNT SINAI THAT GOD FIRST SPOKE FROM THE BURNING BUSH, TELLING ME TO GO AND BRING THE ISRAELITES FROM EGYPT. NOW I HAD RETURNED, BRINGING ALL ISRAEL WITH ME.

THERE WE CAMPED AND WAITED.

ON THE MORNING OF THE THIRD DAY WE WERE WOKEN BY THE SOUND OF THUNDER.

THE MOUNTAIN WAS ALIVE WITH THUNDER AND LIGHTNING — THE NOISE WAS INDESCRIBABLE. PEOPLE WOKE IN TERROR, RUNNING THIS WAY AND THAT, CRYING AND SCREAMING.

AND ALL WERE SAYING THE SAME THING : 'FIND MOSES! WHERE IS MOSES? SAVE US!'

AND THEY HAD GOOD REASON TO BE AFRAID : WITH A TRUMPET BLAST LOUDER THAN THUNDER, GOD HIMSELF HAD COME DOWN ONTO THE MOUNTAIN.

SO I WENT UP THE MOUNTAINSIDE. UP INTO THE SMOKE AND CLOUD, THOUGH THE GROUND TREMBLED AND SMOKE BILLOWED OUT AS FROM A FURNACE.

AND THERE I SAW GOD FACE TO FACE.

AND GOD SPOKE TO ME.

AND THEN I WENT BACK TO THE PEOPLE, AND TOLD THEM EVERYTHING GOD HAD SAID.

AND HE FORGAVE THEM. HE GAVE THEM CHANCE AFTER CHANCE TO ACCEPT HIS WAYS BUT THE ISRAELITES WERE NEVER SATISFIED. AND THEN, WHEN WE WERE WITHIN SIGHT OF THE PROMISED LAND, THE PEOPLE PROVOKED GOD'S ANGER *AGAIN*.

I SENT TWELVE SPIES TO SURVEY THE LAND AHEAD. CALEB, FROM THE TRIBE OF JUDAH, AND JOSHUA, REPORTED THAT THE LAND WAS JUST AS GOD SAID IT WOULD BE.

PEOPLE FLED IN TERROR WHENEVER THEY SAW THEM BECAUSE OF WHAT OUR GOD HAD DONE. THE PEOPLE WE WOULD HAVE TO FIGHT WERE FAINTING AT THE SIGHT OF US!

BUT THE OTHER SPIES EXAGGERATED AND LIED, SAYING THE PEOPLE THERE WERE TOO STRONG FOR US, AND THE LAND TOO POOR TO SUSTAIN LIFE. ALL THAT NIGHT WE ARGUED WITH THEM...

JOSHUA AND CALEB SAY THE LAND HERE IS GOOD. IF IT PLEASES GOD, HE WILL LEAD US INTO THE LAND HE PROMISED US.

BUT WE'LL HAVE TO FIGHT! WE'LL DIE IN BATTLE, OUR WIVES AND CHILDREN WILL BE KIDNAPPED! I SAY WE SHOULD GO BACK TO EGYPT!

EGYPT?! BUT WE HAVE NOTHING TO FEAR! IF GOD IS WITH US, THEN THESE PEOPLE CAN DO NOTHING AGAINST US!

WE DON'T CARE. PEOPLE SAY THERE ARE GIANTS ROAMING LOOSE, AND WE'RE LIKE GRASSHOPPERS TO THEM! OUR LEADERS HAVE LED US TO CERTAIN DEATH. STONE THEM! STONE THEM TO DEATH, APPOINT NEW LEADERS AND RETURN TO EGYPT!

YOU WERE *SLAVES* IN EGYPT! HAVE YOU FORGOTTEN ALREADY WHAT GOD HAS DONE FOR YOU?

IS YOUR FAITH SO WEAK? I WILL APPEAL TO GOD TO SAVE YOUR LIVES.

ENOUGH!

GOD SENTENCED THE UNBELIEVING ISRAELITES TO WANDER IN THE DESERT UNTIL THAT WHOLE GENERATION HAD DIED.

JERICHO IS YOURS. AS LONG AS YOU FOLLOW GOD'S INSTRUCTIONS TO THE LETTER, ITS WALLS WILL CRUMBLE BEFORE YOU.

LISTEN CAREFULLY TO WHAT YOU MUST DO:

MARCH YOUR MEN AROUND THE CITY ONCE A DAY FOR SIX DAYS. SEVEN PRIESTS CARRYING TRUMPETS ARE TO WALK AHEAD OF THE ARK OF THE COVENANT. ON THE SEVENTH DAY MARCH SEVEN TIMES ROUND – WITH THE PRIESTS BLOWING THEIR TRUMPETS.

LET THE WHOLE ARMY GIVE A GREAT SHOUT. THEN THE WALLS WILL COLLAPSE AND YOUR MEN WILL BE FREE TO ENTER.

THE CITY WILL BE YOURS.

JOSHUA GOT UP EARLY THE NEXT MORNING, AND SUMMONED THE PRIESTS WHO HAD CARRIED THE ARK.

DESPITE THE STRANGE INSTRUCTIONS FROM THE COMMANDER OF GOD'S ARMY, JOSHUA TRUSTED GOD COMPLETELY.

AND SO THEY MARCHED AROUND THE CITY, THE SOLDIERS IN THE LEAD, FOLLOWED BY THE SEVEN PRIESTS BLOWING THE TRUMPETS, THE PRIESTS CARRYING THE ARK, AND A REARGUARD OF TROOPS BEHIND THEM.

AROUND THE CITY THEY MARCHED, EVERY DAY FOR SIX DAYS, THE SOLDIERS MARCHING IN THE SHADOW OF THE DEFENCES, THE SOUND OF TRUMPETS ECHOING OFF THE UNYIELDING WALLS. EVERY DAY FOR A WHOLE WEEK THEY MARCHED, BENEATH THE WATCHING EYES OF THE DEFENDERS.

IT WOULD BE FAIR TO SAY THAT THIS WASN'T REALLY WHAT THE SOLDIERS ON THE BATTLEMENTS OF JERICHO WERE EXPECTING...

HERE THEY COME AGAIN.

THIS IS THE SEVENTH TIME THIS WEEK. WHAT ARE THEY DOING OUT THERE? ALL THAT WANDERING AROUND IN THE DESERT MUST HAVE ADDLED THEIR BRAINS!

WHAT'S THE MATTER, TOO SCARED TO FIGHT?

DON'T YOU KNOW ANY OTHER TUNES? YOU'RE STARTING TO BORE US!

WHY DON'T YOU SHOW US WHAT'S IN THE BOX YOU'RE CARRYING? IT'S GOT TO BE MORE INTERESTING THAN LISTENING TO THIS ALL WEEK!

THE PEOPLE DID AS JOSHUA COMMANDED. AND WHEN THE PRIESTS BLEW THE TRUMPETS, THE ARMY GAVE A GREAT SHOUT –

AND AT THAT MOMENT, THE WALLS STARTED TO CRUMBLE...

AND THE WALLS...

CAME TUMBLING DOWN.

AT ONCE, JOSHUA'S ARMY SWEPT UP INTO THE CITY, KILLING EVERYONE AND EVERYTHING IN THEIR SIGHT.

MEN AND WOMEN, OLD PEOPLE AND CHILDREN, CATTLE, SHEEP, EVEN THE DONKEYS IN THE STABLES ; ALL FELL TO THE SWORDS OF THE ISRAELITES.

BUT JOSHUA REMEMBERED THE PROMISES MADE TO RAHAB, AND SO SHE AND HER FAMILY WERE LED TO A PLACE OF SAFETY, OUT OF THE VIOLENCE AND DESTRUCTION.

EXCEPT FOR THE PROSTITUTE AND HER FAMILY, EVERY LIVING THING IN JERICHO WAS SLAUGHTERED.

THAT NIGHT, JERICHO WAS BURNED TO THE GROUND.

THE ARMIES OF THIRTY-ONE KINGS FELL BEFORE JOSHUA'S ARMY, THE SHRINES OF THE PAGAN IDOLS *DESTROYED*. THE PROMISED LAND WAS TO BE HOME TO A PEOPLE CHOSEN BY A GOD WHO TOLERATES NO RIVALS.

THE ISRAELITES PUT AN END TO THE CHILD SACRIFICE AND THE SHRINE PROSTITUTES, TO THE EVIL THAT LAY ON THE LAND.

AND THEN JOSHUA SPOKE TO THE PEOPLE ONE LAST TIME. NEVER AGAIN WOULD ALL ISRAEL BE GATHERED IN ONE PLACE. THESE WERE HIS WORDS:

'THIS IS WHAT THE LORD, OUR GOD, SAYS: "LONG AGO YOUR FATHERS LIVED FAR BEYOND THE RIVER EUPHRATES AND WORSHIPPED STRANGE GODS. BUT I TOOK YOUR FATHER, *ABRAHAM*, AND BROUGHT HIM TO THIS LAND, CALLED *CANAAN*.

'"I GAVE HIM *ISAAC*, AND TO ISAAC HIS SONS *ESAU* AND *JACOB*, BUT JACOB WENT TO EGYPT. SO I SENT *MOSES*, AND I BROUGHT YOU OUT! YOU SAW WITH YOUR *OWN EYES* WHAT I DID TO THE EGYPTIANS!"

'THROW AWAY THE GODS YOUR FATHERS WORSHIPPED BEYOND EUPHRATES AND IN EGYPT. AND SERVE GOD ONLY. CHOOSE *NOW* WHOM YOU WILL SERVE.

'AS FOR ME AND MY FAMILY, WE WILL SERVE THE LORD.'

THE PEOPLE CHOSE GOD THAT DAY, AS JOSHUA CHOSE, AND THE TWELVE TRIBES WENT EACH TO THE SECTION OF LAND THAT JOSHUA HAD APPORTIONED. JOSEPH'S BONES, CARRIED FROM EGYPT, WERE BURIED.

THEY WERE HOME AT LAST...

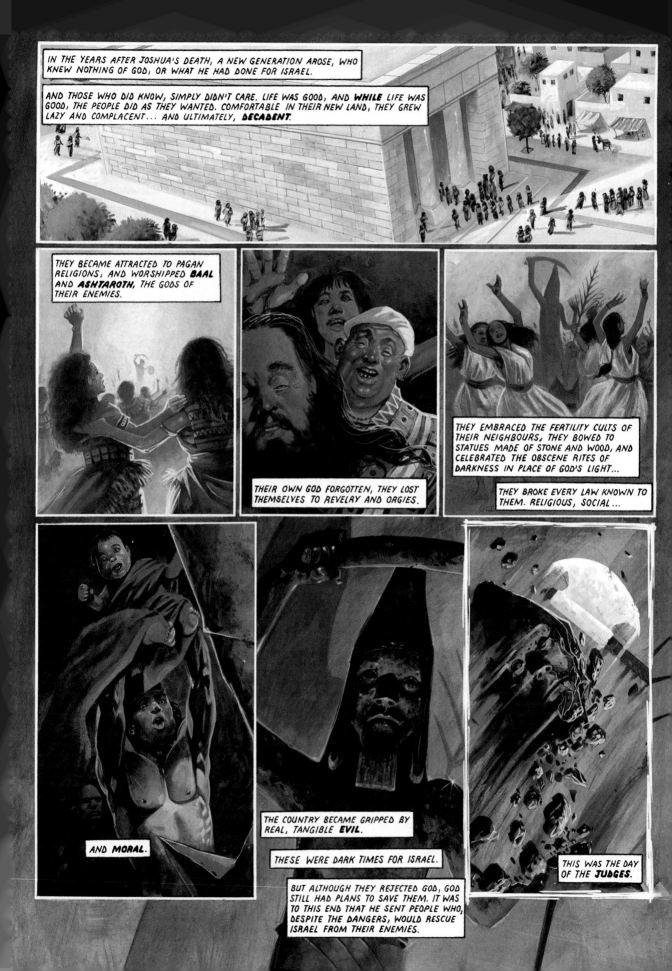

IN THE YEARS AFTER JOSHUA'S DEATH, A NEW GENERATION AROSE, WHO KNEW NOTHING OF GOD, OR WHAT HE HAD DONE FOR ISRAEL.

AND THOSE WHO DID KNOW, SIMPLY DIDN'T CARE. LIFE WAS GOOD, AND **WHILE** LIFE WAS GOOD, THE PEOPLE DID AS THEY WANTED. COMFORTABLE IN THEIR NEW LAND, THEY GREW LAZY AND COMPLACENT... AND ULTIMATELY, **DECADENT**.

THEY BECAME ATTRACTED TO PAGAN RELIGIONS, AND WORSHIPPED **BAAL** AND **ASHTAROTH**, THE GODS OF THEIR ENEMIES.

THEIR OWN GOD FORGOTTEN, THEY LOST THEMSELVES TO REVELRY AND ORGIES.

THEY EMBRACED THE FERTILITY CULTS OF THEIR NEIGHBOURS, THEY BOWED TO STATUES MADE OF STONE AND WOOD, AND CELEBRATED THE OBSCENE RITES OF DARKNESS IN PLACE OF GOD'S LIGHT...

THEY BROKE EVERY LAW KNOWN TO THEM. RELIGIOUS, SOCIAL...

AND **MORAL**.

THE COUNTRY BECAME GRIPPED BY REAL, TANGIBLE **EVIL**.

THESE WERE DARK TIMES FOR ISRAEL.

BUT ALTHOUGH THEY REJECTED GOD, GOD STILL HAD PLANS TO SAVE THEM. IT WAS TO THIS END THAT HE SENT PEOPLE WHO, DESPITE THE DANGERS, WOULD RESCUE ISRAEL FROM THEIR ENEMIES.

THIS WAS THE DAY OF THE **JUDGES**.

THE STORY OF SAMSON

OOR SAMSON. IF HE KNEW SHE SECRETLY SERVED HER PHILISTINE MASTERS, HE DIDN'T CARE. AFTER ALL, HE WAS **SAMSON** — HAT COULD HARM HIM?

HEY OFFERED HER A FORTUNE, IF ONLY HE WOULD FIND THE SECRET OF HIS STRENGTH, AND THE WAY TO ROB HIM OF IT. AND SO SHE BEGAN...

WHY WON'T YOU TELL ME YOUR SECRET? YOU WOULD IF YOU REALLY LOVED ME.

IT'S NO SECRET. TIE ME UP WITH SOGGY BOWSTRINGS AND I'LL BE LIKE A KITTEN.

YOU'RE LAUGHING AT ME!

I'M SORRY. ONLY UNUSED ROPE CAN HOLD ME AND —

WHY DO YOU KEEP LYING?

ALL RIGHT THE TRUTH — WEAVE MY HAIR INTO A LOOM AND THEN — WHERE ARE YOU GOING?

IN THE END HE GAVE IN.

IT'S MY HAIR.

E WAS SO PERSISTENT. BUT EN SHE WOULD BE — THEY'D FERED HER A **FORTUNE**.

HIS STRENGTH CAME FROM GOD.

HIS LONG HAIR WAS A SYMBOL, A SIGN OF HIS DEVOTION. IF HIS HAIR WAS CUT, GOD WOULD TAKE HIS STRENGTH AWAY.

HE SHOULD NEVER HAVE TOLD HER, BECAUSE WHILE HE SLEPT (WORN OUT BY HER CONSTANT NAGGING, NO DOUBT). SHE CUT OFF ALL HIS HAIR.

YOU CAN'T IMAGINE HOW MUCH THE PHILISTINES HATED SAMSON. THEY GOUGED HIS EYES OUT AND MADE HIM WORK LIKE A COMMON OX.

NOW, THE PHILISTINES WORSHIPPED A GOD THEY CALLED DAGON, AND WITH SAMSON NOT ONLY THEIR PRISONER, BUT UTTERLY HUMILIATED INTO THE BARGAIN, THEY DECIDED TO HOLD A GREAT FEAST IN CELEBRATION, TO THANK THEIR GOD.

WAS ALL HE HAD LEFT OF HIS VOWS A NAZARITE. HE'D ALREADY BROKEN E OTHERS, AND NOW THAT HE HAD LOWED THIS WOMAN TO CUT HIS HAIR, WAS NO DIFFERENT FROM ANYONE SE.

HE WAS NO STRONGER THAN AN ORDINARY MAN. AND THE PHILISTINES CAPTURED HIM JUST AS EASILY.

HE HAD ONCE BEEN ISRAEL'S DEFENDER, CHOSEN BY GOD HIMSELF! NOW HE WAS NO BETTER THAN A FARM ANIMAL.

THE STORY OF SAMUEL

WHEN JOSHUA LED THE PEOPLE INTO THE PROMISED LAND, HE SENT THE ARK OF THE COVENANT TO A PLACE CALLED **SHILOH**, AND THERE IT STAYED FOR ALMOST TWO HUNDRED YEARS.

ISRAEL HAD NO TEMPLES, BUT THE ARK WAS KEPT IN A LARGE TENT, TENDED BY A FAMILY OF PRIESTS, RESPONSIBILITY PASSING FROM FATHER TO SON. EVEN WHEN PEOPLE TREATED GOD WITH CONTEMPT, SHILOH STAYED AS THE FOCUS OF RELIGIOUS LIFE.

EVENTUALLY THE FESTIVALS BECAME MERE SOCIAL EVENTS, DEVOID OF ANY REAL MEANING.

EVERY YEAR PEOPLE WOULD TRAVEL UP TO SHILOH TO WORSHIP GOD AND MAKE SACRIFICES. AMONG THEM, AT THIS TIME, CAME A MAN NAMED ELKANAH, WITH HIS TWO WIVES, PENINNAH AND HANNAH.

AND IT IS WITH **HANNAH** THAT OUR STORY STARTS. ALTHOUGH ELKANAH'S OTHER WIFE HAD CHILDREN, HANNAH HAD NONE...

HAA—HAA!

AND PENINNAH WAS CRUEL, AND TEASED HANNAH MERCILESSLY.

YOU SHOULDN'T LET HER UPSET YOU HANNAH.

I'M NOT UPSET.

THEN WHY ARE YOU CRYING? SHE'S JUST JEALOUS. SHE KNOWS THAT I LOVE YOU MORE THAN HER, AND IT'S **TRUE**, I DO! WHAT DOES IT MATTER IF SHE HAS **TEN** SONS, I —

HANNAH? HAVE I SAID SOMETHING WRONG?

IT ALWAYS COMES BACK TO THAT, DOESN'T IT? I'M GOING TO THE TEMPLE! I'LL TALK TO YOU LATER!

OH, LORD GOD! IF ONLY YOU WOULD SEE MY MISERY AND GIVE ME JUST ONE SON, THEN I WOULD GIVE HIM BACK TO YOU FOR THE REST OF HIS LIFE!

NO SIR! I WAS PRAYING!

AND AS ELI THE PRIEST SAID THESE WORDS, HANNAH FELT A GREAT SENSE OF **GLADNESS**. SHE SOMEHOW KNEW THAT GOD HAD HEARD HER PRAYERS, AND THAT THEY HAD BEEN ANSWERED!

WHAT'S THIS? ANOTHER DRUNK?!

HOW MANY TIMES MUST I **TELL** YOU PEOPLE! THIS IS THE HOUSE OF **GOD**! YOU CAN'T COME IN **HERE** TO SLEEP OFF YOUR HANGOVER!

PRAYING?! FORGIVE ME. IT'S... WELL, IT'S BEEN A GOOD MANY YEARS SINCE I SAW SOMEONE DO **THAT** IN HERE. PRAYING, EH?

NOW THERE'S A THING...

WELL, MAY GOD BLESS YOU, CHILD. GO IN PEACE, AND MAY GOD **GIVE** YOU WHATEVER IT IS YOU WERE ASKING FOR!

SURE ENOUGH, SOON HANNAH BECAME PREGNANT AND GAVE BIRTH TO A SON, CALLED **SAMUEL**.

THOUGH SHE HAD WAITED SO MANY YEARS FOR A BABY, SHE KNEW THAT SHE MUST KEEP HER PROMISE TO GOD. HER TIME WITH SAMUEL WOULD BE VERY SHORT...

WHEN HE WAS OLD ENOUGH, SHE BROUGHT THE CHILD TO **ELI**, THE PRIEST...

I ASKED GOD FOR THIS CHILD, AND GOD GAVE HIM TO ME. NOW I GIVE HIM BACK — TO SERVE GOD FOR HIS WHOLE LIFE.

I SEE. AND WHAT DOES YOUR HUSBAND THINK OF THIS?

I SAY SHE SHOULD DO AS SHE THINKS BEST.

I MADE GOD A PROMISE, AND NOW I MUST KEEP IT. TAKE CARE OF HIM, FOR I LOVE HIM SO MUCH!

AND SO THE BOY SAMUEL SERVED THE LORD GOD.

HE GREW UP IN THE SHADOW OF THE ALTAR, MINISTERING WITH ELI, AND GROWING IN FAVOUR WITH GOD AND THE PEOPLE.

SADLY THE SAME COULD HARDLY BE SAID OF ELI'S **OWN** SONS...

ALTHOUGH THEY WOULD BE THE SPIRITUAL LEADERS OF THE NATION AFTER HIS DEATH, THEY DIDN'T CARE ABOUT GOD, THEIR DUTIES, OR ANYTHING BUT THEMSELVES!

LOOK IT'S (BURP) SAMM-UEL! SHUCH A NICE LAD!

I'LL DRINK TO THAT!

EVERY NIGHT, SAMUEL SLEPT IN THE TENT OF MEETING, NEAR THE ARK ITSELF. ONE NIGHT, AS HE LAY SLEEPING, SOMETHING **STRANGE** HAPPENED. HE HEARD A **VOICE**, CALLING HIM...

SAMUEL!

SAMUEL!

YOU CALLED ME, ELI! WHAT'S WRONG?

YOU'RE HAVING BAD DREAMS, BOY. NOW GO BACK TO BED, I DIDN'T CALL FOR YOU, AND YOU'VE A BUSY DAY TOMORROW.

SAMUEL DID AS HE WAS TOLD, BUT TEN MINUTES LATER...

ELI, YOU CALLED ME! I HEARD IT!

WELL IT WASN'T ME. THERE'S NO ONE HERE EXCEPT YOU AND I, AND IT CERTAINLY WASN'T **ME.**

GO BACK TO SLEEP, LAD.

96

THE YEARS PASSED BY.

SAMUEL WAS THE LAST OF THE GREAT JUDGES, AND HE LED HIS PEOPLE OUT FROM THE CHAOS OF THOSE DAYS.

HE URGED THEM TO ABANDON THE FOREIGN GODS, AND TO SEEK FORGIVENESS FOR THEIR UNHOLY PRACTICES.

THERE WAS PEACE IN ISRAEL AS THE HOSTILE PHILISTINES WERE SUBDUED, AND ISRAEL MADE PEACE WITH THE NEIGHBOURING AMORITES.

AND THROUGHOUT IT ALL THERE WAS SAMUEL, PRAYING DAY AND NIGHT, AND ADMINISTERING JUSTICE.

YEAR IN, YEAR OUT, HE TRAVELLED THE COUNTRY, SETTLING DISPUTES WITH HONESTY AND FAIRNESS. BUT ALWAYS HE RETURNED TO THE TOWN OF **RAMAH**, WHICH HE HAD MADE HIS HOME.

THE YEARS WENT BY. SAMUEL GREW OLD.

AND IT WAS TO RAMAH, THAT THE ELDERS OF ALL ISRAEL GATHERED, TO BRING SAMUEL UNBELIEVABLE NEWS...

SAMUEL, YOU HAVE LED US WELL THESE LAST YEARS, NO ONE CAN DENY IT. BUT YOU WON'T BE WITH US FOREVER, AND FRANKLY, WE WORRY ABOUT THE FUTURE.

WE HAVE DECIDED WE WANT TO BE LIKE OTHER COUNTRIES. WE WANT A **KING** !

98

LONG LIVE THE KING! LONG LIVE THE KING!

IT WAS JUST WHAT THE PEOPLE HAD WANTED.

ANY CRITICS OF THE NEW RULER WERE SILENCED BY SAUL'S SUCCESS AS A MILITARY LEADER.

BEFORE HE WAS EVEN CONFIRMED AS KING, SAUL LIBERATED THE CITY OF JABESH, CAPTURED BY THE AMMONITES.

THE NATION UNITED BEHIND SAUL.

SAUL LED THE PEOPLE TO VICTORY AFTER VICTORY. ENEMIES THAT HAD THREATENED ISRAEL FOR YEARS WERE SWIFTLY DEALT WITH.

SAUL MUSTERED THE ARMY AGAINST THE PHILISTINES, BUT SAMUEL SENT WORD TO WAIT SEVEN DAYS BEFORE ATTACKING, SO THAT HE MIGHT COME AND OFFER THE REQUIRED SACRIFICES TO GOD.

BUT SAUL WOULD NOT WAIT...

SIR! WE'VE BEEN HERE SIX DAYS NOW AND STILL NO WORD! LET US ATTACK NOW OR LEAVE!

SOMETHING MUST HAVE HAPPENED TO SAMUEL TO DELAY HIM. I DON'T LIKE THIS AT ALL.

SAUL WAS THEIR KING AND ALL THE WHILE IN THE BACKGROUND THERE WAS **SAMUEL** - EVER FAITHFUL, WATCHING AND GUIDING.

BUT THERE WAS A PRICE. GOD HAD CHOSEN SAUL AS A HUMBLE MAN, BUT SOON HE WAS CONSUMED WITH ARROGANCE...

PREPARE THE OFFERINGS. THERE'S NOTHING FOR IT: I MUST DO THE SACRIFICES MYSELF!

BUT SIR, SAMUEL HAS ALWAYS –

GOD SPEAKS TO SAMUEL, SAMUEL SPEAKS TO ME, IT'S ALL THE SAME THING. NOW HURRY! LET'S GET THE SACRIFICES OVER WITH SO WE CAN GET ON WITH THE BATTLE!

SAUL!

AH, SAMUEL! THERE YOU ARE! I WAS STARTING TO WORRY ABOUT YOU.

I THOUGHT YOU WEREN'T COMIN' SO I'VE DONE THE OFFERINGS MYSELF!

YOU WERE TOLD TO WAIT! THE INSTRUCTION CAME FROM **GOD**, NOT ME!

IF YOU HAD ONLY DONE AS YOU WERE TOLD, YOUR KINGDOM WOULD HAVE LASTED FOR EVER!

AND NOW?

GOD WILL FIND ANOTHER. SOMEONE AFTER HIS OWN HEART.

AND FROM THAT MOMENT, SAUL STARTED TO CHANGE...

SAUL AND HIS SON, **JONATHAN**, DEFEATED THE PHILISTINES THAT DAY. DESPITE SAMUEL'S WORDS, THE VICTORIES STILL CAME THICK AND FAST.

THEN SAUL RECEIVED WORD FROM SAMUEL THAT THEY WERE TO ATTACK THE AMALEKITES. GOD HAD HIS OWN REASONS, AND SAUL WAS TO OBEY.

THE AMALEKITES WERE TO BE COMPLETELY WIPED OUT, EVEN THEIR CATTLE AND SHEEP MUST DIE.

AND SO SAUL DID ALL THAT GOD HAD SAID.

WITH ONE OR TWO EXCEPTIONS...

AGAG, KING OF THE AMALEKITES! I'VE DECIDED TO LET YOU LIVE. AFTER ALL, THERE ARE NO AMALEKITES LEFT TO RULE, ARE THERE?

WHAT WILL SAMUEL SAY?

I'M SURE HE'LL BE **DELIGHTED**!

ANOTHER VICTORY, SAMUEL. MAY GOD BLESS YOU, FOR I HAVE CARRIED OUT YOUR INSTRUCTIONS TO THE LETTER.

TO THE LETTER, EH? THEN WHY DO I HEAR THE BLEATING OF SHEEP? WHY CAN I HEAR COWS MOOING? WHY IS YOUR CAMP FULL OF HERDS OF ANIMALS?!

IT SEEMED A WASTE TO KILL THEM. SO WE SAVED THE BEST SHEEP AND CATTLE, AND I'M GOING TO SACRIFICE THEM ALL TO YOUR GOD!

STOP! I DON'T WANT TO **HEAR** ANY OF THIS!

THE STORY OF DAVID

104

THE KING HIMSELF!

THIS IS *ABSURD*, YOUR MAJESTY! IF THE MEN ARE ALL TOO SCARED, *I'LL* GO AND FIGHT HIM FOR YOU!

SIR! WITH *RESPECT*, I'VE LOOKED AFTER MY FATHER'S SHEEP FOR YEARS. IF THEY WERE ATTACKED, I'D DEFEND THEM! I'VE FOUGHT LIONS AND BEARS. WHY SHOULD THIS PHILISTINE *DOG* BE ANY DIFFERENT?

SO I TOLD HIM, 'GOD DELIVERED ME FROM LIONS AND BEARS, HE'LL DELIVER ME FROM GOLIATH.' AND THAT SEEMED TO PERSUADE HIM. HE SUMMONED HIS ARMOURERS AND HAD ME DRESSED FOR BATTLE THERE AND THEN.

NO ONE DOUBTS YOUR BRAVERY, ER... *DAVID*, IS IT? BUT YOU MUST FACE *FACTS*. GOLIATH IS A *GIANT*, AND THERE ISN'T A MAN IN THE ARMY WHO COULD HOPE TO DEFEAT HIM IN BATTLE. I MEAN, HAVE YOU *SEEN* HOW BIG HE IS?

SAUL GAVE ME HIS OWN ARMOUR TO WEAR. IT WAS RIDICULOUS. I COULD HARDLY *MOVE* IN THE STUFF, IT WAS SO HEAVY! I COULDN'T EVEN LIFT SAUL'S *SWORD*! IN THE END I DECIDED I'D BE BETTER OFF WITHOUT IT.

'HA', I SAID. 'YOU'VE COME ARMED WITH A SPEAR, BUT I'M HERE IN THE NAME OF *GOD*'!

WHEN GOLIATH FINALLY CLAPPED EYES ON ME, HE WENT *BERSERK*! I WASN'T WHAT HE HAD BEEN EXPECTING...

YOU'RE SENDING A *BOY*?! DO YOU THINK I'M A *DOG*, AND HAVE SENT A BOY WITH A STICK TO CHASE ME OFF? COME ANY CLOSER AND I'LL TEAR YOUR *SKIN* OFF!

SO GOLIATH STARTED CHARGING DOWN THE HILL TOWARDS ME, SHOUTING AND SWEARING ALL THE WAY.

I PUT A PEBBLE IN THE SLING I USED TO SCARE AWAY WOLVES AND, WHIRLING IT HIGH IN THE AIR, I LET FLY AS HARD AS I COULD!

WHACK!

STRAIGHT BETWEEN THE EYES! THE GIANT WENT DOWN LIKE A FELLED TREE.

SO I TOOK THE GIANT'S GREAT BIG SWORD, AND HACKED HIS **HEAD** OFF! THEN I GAVE IT TO KING SAUL AS A PRESENT.

TRUST GOD - FIND OUT FOR YOURSELF HOW GOOD GOD IS, EVEN LIONS AND WOLVES GROW WEAK AND HUNGRY, BUT THIS POOR MAN CALLED AND GOD ANSWERED HIM.

AND SO I WENT TO LIVE WITH THE KING. I PLAYED THE HARP AND SANG, AND MY SONGS SEEMED TO SOOTHE HIS BLACK MOODS.

BUT RIGHT FROM THE START, SAUL WAS AFRAID OF ME.

HE TAUGHT ME TO FIGHT WITH A SWORD, AND I QUICKLY LEARNED HOW TO DEFEND MYSELF IN BATTLE.

AGAIN AND AGAIN GOD GAVE ME VICTORY IN THE CAMPAIGNS I LED AGAINST OUR ENEMIES. BUT SAUL'S FEAR TURNED TO JEALOUSY...

HURRAH FOR **DAVID**! SAUL HAS KILLED **THOUSANDS**! BUT DAVID HAS KILLED **TENS** OF THOUSANDS!

DAVID!! **DAVID**!! GOD IS **WITH** YOU!!

IF THE PEOPLE ACCEPTED ME, IT WAS BECAUSE **GOD** HAD PUT HIS POWER IN ME.

SAUL'S SON **JONATHAN** AND I BECAME LIKE BROTHERS. HE GAVE ME HIS OWN WEAPONS, HIS OWN SWORD. WE FOUGHT SIDE BY SIDE AND I WOULD HAVE GLADLY **DIED** FOR HIM.

OUR FRIENDSHIP MADE SAUL ALL THE MORE JEALOUS. AND HIS JEALOUSY TURNED TO RAGE...

STAY **STILL**!! I'M THE **KING**! I **COMMAND** IT!

LUCKILY HIS AIM WASN'T WHAT IT ONCE HAD BEEN!

THAT NIGHT THE KING HAD HIS SERVANTS KEEP WATCH. HE WOULD KILL ME NEXT DAY.

BUT MICHAL, MY WIFE AND SAUL'S OWN **DAUGHTER**, HELPED ME ESCAPE. IN ALL ISRAEL, IT SEEMED AS IF THE KING WAS THE **ONLY** MAN WHO HATED ME!

JERUSALEM!

I WAS THIRTY YEARS OLD WHEN I BECAME KING. I UNITED THE WARRING TRIBES, AND TOGETHER WE LAID SIEGE TO THE CITY THAT WOULD BEAR MY NAME:

DAVID'S CITY —

THE RULING JEBUSITES KNEW THEY WERE WELL DEFENDED BEHIND ITS WALLS —

THEY SHOUTED: 'EVEN THE BLIND AND CRIPPLED COULD HOLD THIS CITY.'

OUCH! MY HEAD! COULDN'T WE JUST STORM THE WALLS LIKE LAST TIME?

SHUT UP AND KEEP CRAWLING!

AND THAT'S EXACTLY HOW WE CONQUERED IT. CRAWLING ALONG THE TUNNELS BENEATH THE CITY ON OUR HANDS AND KNEES IN THE DARKNESS, WE LEAPT OUT TO TAKE THEM BY SURPRISE!

WAS IT A HARD BATTLE?

HARD? THERE ARE NO EASY BATTLES. PEOPLE FIGHT, PEOPLE DIE. IF IT'S GOD'S WILL, WE WIN. IF NOT... WELL, THIS BATTLE WAS GOD'S WILL ANYWAY.

THE CITY WAS OURS!

I HAD THE ARK BROUGHT UP TO THE CITY. ALL ISRAEL TURNED OUT TO GREET IT, SINGING AND DANCING, AND SHOUTING..!

IT WAS WONDERFUL! FROM NOW ONWARDS, JERUSALEM WOULD BE OUR HOME, THE PLACE WHERE WE WOULD BUILD THE TEMPLE OF OUR GOD.

I DANCED IN FRONT OF THE PEOPLE, STRIPPED DOWN TO A LOINCLOTH. I WAS WITH THE PEOPLE, ONE OF THEM! LEAPING AND DANCING BEFORE OUR GOD, BECAUSE WE WERE SO HAPPY! HE LIVED WITH US! NOT A GOD OF WOOD OR STONE, BUT ALIVE!

OF COURSE, MY WIFE DIDN'T LIKE IT. SAID IT WAS UNDIGNIFIED, ALL THAT PRANCING ABOUT AND SHOUTING - NOT FIT BEHAVIOUR FOR A KING. BAH! I WASN'T DOING IT FOR HER!

IT WAS THEN THAT GOD TOLD ME THE NEWS THAT ONE OF MY HEIRS WOULD BUILD A KINGDOM THAT WOULD LAST FOREVER. AND ALTHOUGH PUNISHED BY THE WHIPS OF MEN, GOD WOULD BE HIS FATHER, AND HE WOULD BE HIS SON, AND HIS KINGDOM WOULD HAVE NO END...

ALL THIS, FROM AN HEIR TO MY THRONE, DESPITE THE SINS I COMMITTED. AND I KNOW THE WRONG I'VE DONE TO OTHERS. I HAVE BEEN SINFUL FROM THE TIME MY MOTHER CONCEIVED ME, EVEN BEFORE I WAS BORN.

AND MY SINS WERE THE MOST **UNORIGINAL**.

IT WAS SPRING, THE TIME WHEN KINGS GO OFF TO WAR. I WAS LOOKING DOWN FROM THE PALACE ROOF WHEN I **SAW** HER.

OH, I HAD WIVES ENOUGH ALREADY. I HAD SONS AND DAUGHTERS, ALL THAT A MAN COULD WANT.

EVERYTHING EXCEPT **HER**.

SHE WAS CALLED **BATHSHEBA**.

SHE WAS BEAUTIFUL.

SHE WAS ENCHANTING.

SHE WAS ENOUGH TO MAKE ME LOSE MY MIND WITH DESIRE.

SHE WAS ANOTHER MAN'S WIFE.

AND I DIDN'T **CARE**.

URIAH, HER HUSBAND WAS A **HITTITE**, ONE OF MY SPECIAL GUARD, AND AWAY FIGHTING MY WARS. UNDER LAW, SOLDIERS WERE NOT ALLOWED TO RETURN TO THEIR WIVES WHILE ON ACTIVE DUTY, AND HE WAS A MAN OF GREAT PRINCIPLE. WHILE HE SLEPT IN TENTS BENEATH THE CITY WALLS OF RABBAH I MADE LOVE TO HIS WIFE IN MY PALACE.

BATHSHEBA BECAME PREGNANT. **FOOL** THAT I WAS, I COVERED ONE EVIL WITH **ANOTHER** - I SENT URIAH ON A DANGEROUS MISSION, AND GAVE ORDERS FOR HIM TO BE LEFT **STRANDED** WHERE THE FIGHTING WAS THE THICKEST.

IT WAS AS IF I'D MURDERED HIM **MYSELF**.

AND SO, AS I SAT THERE THINKING I'D GOT AWAY WITH THINGS, I WAS VISITED BY *NATHAN*, A HIGHLY RESPECTED PROPHET...

WHOEVER IT WAS, HE DESERVES TO *DIE*!

I SWEAR BY GOD, THAT WHOEVER DID THIS SHOULD PAY BACK *FOUR TIMES* AS MUCH, BECAUSE OF HIS CRUELTY!

OF COURSE, NATHAN WAS REALLY TALKING ABOUT *ME*. GOD *MADE* ME KING OVER ISRAEL, HE *GAVE* ME MY KINGDOM, MY WIVES, *EVERYTHING*. IF I'D SAID IT WASN'T *ENOUGH*, THEN HE'D HAVE *GIVEN* ME EVEN MORE!

THERE ARE TWO MEN IN YOUR KINGDOM. ONE IS *RICH* AND OWNS WHOLE HERDS OF SHEEP, WHILE THE OTHER OWNS *NOTHING* BUT ONE SMALL LAMB, WHICH HE HAS RAISED SINCE BIRTH. IT'S ALL HE HAS IN THE *WORLD*, YET THE RICH MAN *TOOK* IT FROM HIM TO SERVE TO A GUEST, RATHER THAN SLAUGHTER ONE OF HIS OWN FLOCK.

INSTEAD I STOLE FROM SOMEONE ELSE, AND *MURDERED* TO COVER MY CRIME.

I WAS A FOOL TO THINK I COULD HIDE FROM GOD, OR THAT MY SIN WOULD GO UNPUNISHED. THE CHILD BATHSHEBA WAS BEARING *DIED*. EVEN SO, GOD HONOURED HIS PROMISE OF A DESCENDANT WHO WOULD RULE FOR EVER. SOON BATHSHEBA GAVE BIRTH TO ANOTHER SON. I NAMED HIM *SOLOMON* AND THANKED GOD THAT I HAD BEEN FORGIVEN...

I HAD OTHER SONS BY OTHER WIVES. MY ELDEST SON, *ABSALOM* HATED HIS HALF-BROTHER AMNON WITH A VENGEANCE.

FATHER, I'M HAVING MY ENTIRE HERD SHEARED. COME AND JOIN ME IN THE CELEBRATIONS — BRING ALL MY BROTHERS, ALL YOUR COURTIERS! BE MY GUESTS.

NOT NOW ABSALOM — WE'RE BUSY. MAYBE NEXT YEAR, MM?

IT WAS *TERRIBLE*! AMNON HAD FALLEN IN LOVE WITH HIS HALF-SISTER TAMAR, AND IN HIS LUST HE *RAPED* HER. AFTER THE ATTACK, HE WANTED NOTHING MORE TO DO WITH HER, AND HAD HER THROWN FROM HIS HOUSE.

NO! YOU MUST ALL COME *NOW*!

'MUST'?

THIS IS *IMPORTANT* TO ME!

ABSALOM SOUGHT ONLY REVENGE FROM THAT MOMENT ON...

I DON'T UNDERSTAND, ABSALOM. WHY ALL THIS FUSS NOW? YOU'VE NEVER BOTHERED WITH PARTIES *BEFORE*?

IF YOU'RE *DETERMINED* TO MAKE ME LOOK STUPID, THEN FINE. BUT AT LEAST LET MY HALF-BROTHER *AMNON* COME!

ABSALOM, MY OWN SON, KILLED HIS HALF-BROTHER AND THEN FLED TO THE LAND OF A FOREIGN KING. EVEN SO, I MISSED HIM TERRIBLY. IN THE END I HAD TO FORGIVE HIM AND HE RETURNED TO ME, ALTHOUGH I REFUSED EVEN TO BE IN THE SAME *ROOM* AS HIM FOR THE FIRST TWO YEARS.

HE WAS WITHOUT DOUBT, THE MOST HANDSOME MAN IN ALL OF ISRAEL. PEOPLE WOULD DO *ANYTHING* FOR HIM.

I WAS BLIND TO HIS AMBITIONS, EVEN THEN. I NEVER LOOKED PROPERLY, OR LISTENED PROPERLY, NEVER KNEW HOW FAR HE WAS WILLING TO GO...

IF IT WILL SHUT YOU UP, CERTAINLY!

THE PARTY WENT *EXACTLY* AS ABSALOM HAD PLANNED IT — HE WAITED UNTIL AMNON WAS DULLED WITH WINE, AND HAD HIS SERVANTS MURDER HIM.

ABSALOM HAD HIS OWN AGENDA.

HE ASKED PERMISSION TO GO TO HEBRON TO WORSHIP GOD. OF COURSE I CONSENTED. BUT AS SOON AS HE WAS OUT OF MY SIGHT, HE HAD HIS TRUMPETS SOUND, GATHERING MEN FROM ALL OVER THE COUNTRY.

AT HEBRON, ABSALOM DECLARED HIMSELF *KING*.

HE SET HIMSELF UP AS A *JUDGE*, OFFERING ADVICE LACED WITH FLATTERY, WINNING FAVOURS FROM THOSE HE HELPED, AND ALWAYS MAKING SURE THEY KNEW THEY OWED HIM.

IT WAS DEBT HE INTENDED THEM TO REPAY *IN FULL*.

HE FORCED ME TO RETREAT UNTIL I COULD GATHER MY FORCES. THEN I SPLIT MY MEN INTO THREE GROUPS AND FACED HIM.

JOAB, MY MILITARY CHIEF TOOK ONE; HIS BROTHER ABISHAI ANOTHER, AND ITTAI, A FOREIGNER WHO OWED ME NOTHING YET REMAINED FAITHFUL, THE THIRD. I GAVE EXPRESS ORDERS THAT ABSALOM WAS TO BE BROUGHT TO ME *UNHARMED*. YOU ASKED IF SOME BATTLES WERE HARD? IN TRUTH, THEN: THIS WAS THE *HARDEST* OF THEM ALL.

THE BATTLE TOOK PLACE IN THE FOREST OF EPHRAIM.

THE FIGHTING WAS CLOSE AND BRUTAL, SWORD AGAINST SWORD, AS EACH MAN STRUGGLED THROUGH THE FOREST.

AND ALL THE WHILE JOAB PUSHED ON, RELENTLESSLY HACKING HIS WAY TOWARDS THE TARGET OF HIS ANGER —

ABSALOM.

I AM THE *KING* NOW! DO YOU HEAR ME?! *THE KING!* *YOU WILL DO AS I COMMAND!*

SURRENDER, IN THE NAME OF KING DAVID! SURRENDER OR DIE!

FOOL! MY FATHER WOULD NEVER HARM ME!

AND SO WITH HIS MEN IN DEFEAT, ABSALOM FLED THE BATTLE, PERHAPS HOPING TO REGROUP AND ATTACK AT A LATER DATE.

WITH JOAB'S TROOPS AT HIS HEELS, HE FLED INTO THE DARKEST PART OF THE FOREST...

I WAS STILL **KING**. I HAD A DUTY TO THE PEOPLE. THERE WOULD BE OTHER BATTLES, OTHER FAILURES, OTHER VICTORIES.

GOD HAS BEEN WITH ME FROM THE DAY HE TOOK ME FROM THE FIELDS, TENDING MY FATHER'S **SHEEP**, AND SET ME UP AS RULER OVER HIS PEOPLE, ISRAEL.

AND AS IF THAT WASN'T ENOUGH, GOD HAS TOLD ME THAT MY ROYAL LINE WILL ENDURE **FOR EVER**.

BELIEVE ME, **I** HAVE DONE NOTHING TO DESERVE THIS HONOUR. THE KING WHO RULES WITH **JUSTICE** IS LIKE A GREAT LIGHT SHINING AFTER THE STORMS. AND **THIS** IS HOW GOD WILL BLESS MY DESCENDANTS - BECAUSE GOD HAS MADE AN **EVERLASTING** AGREEMENT WITH ME.

SOON I WILL GO THE WAY OF ALL THE EARTH. **SOLOMON** WILL SUCCEED ME.

THE LORD GOD IS MY SHEPHERD, I SHALL NEVER WANT. IN GREEN PASTURES HE GIVES ME REST, HE LEADS ME TO THE STILL, FRESH WATERS. HE WILL REVIVE MY SPIRIT AND MY STRENGTH. HE GUIDES ME IN THE PATHS OF RIGHTEOUSNESS.

ALTHOUGH I WALK THROUGH THE VALLEY OF THE SHADOW OF DEATH, I WILL FEAR NO EVIL, FOR HE IS WITH ME. HIS SHEPHERD'S CROOK AND STAFF, THEY COMFORT ME.

SURELY GOODNESS AND LOVE SHALL FOLLOW ME ALL THE DAYS OF MY LIFE, AND I SHALL DWELL IN THE HOUSE OF THE LORD... FOR EVER.

THE STORY OF SOLOMON

SOLOMON WAS THE SON OF DAVID AND **BATHSHEBA**, URIAH'S WIFE. ALTHOUGH NOT THE ELDEST OF DAVID'S SONS, HE WAS CHOSEN TO SUCCEED HIM AS KING.

IN THOSE DAYS THERE WAS NO TEMPLE IN ISRAEL, AND THE ARK OF THE COVENANT STILL RESIDED IN A TENT AS IT HAD DONE FOR HUNDREDS OF YEARS.

ONE NIGHT, AS SOLOMON SLEPT NEAR THE PLACE WHERE SACRIFICES WERE OFFERED, HE HAD A DREAM IN WHICH **GOD** SPOKE TO HIM...

SOLOMON, ASK FOR WHATEVER YOU WANT ME TO GIVE YOU.

YOU SHOWED MY FATHER, DAVID, GREAT KINDNESS ALL HIS LIFE. YOU MADE ME HIS HEIR, BUT I DON'T KNOW HOW TO **RULE** THIS COUNTRY. I FEEL LIKE A CHILD WITH THE WHOLE NATION **WATCHING** ME. GIVE ME AN UNDERSTANDING HEART, TO JUDGE YOUR PEOPLE; GIVE ME THE **WISDOM** TO RULE WITH JUSTICE AND FAIRNESS.

I WILL MAKE YOU THE **WISEST** MAN ON EARTH! I WILL ALSO GIVE YOU THE THINGS YOU DID **NOT** ASK FOR! YOU WILL **HAVE** WEALTH AND POWER AND, IF YOU OBEY ME, YOU WILL LIVE A LONG LIFE TOO!

YOU COULD HAVE ASKED FOR ANYTHING - POWER; WEALTH; A LONG **LIFE** - BUT INSTEAD YOU ASK FOR **WISDOM**.

THEN SOLOMON AWOKE - AND HE REALIZED IT HAD BEEN A DREAM.

AND SO SOLOMON BECAME KING.

THE WISEST, RICHEST, AND MOST REGAL OF ALL THE KINGS OF ISRAEL. IT WAS TO BE A RARE TIME OF **PEACE** AND PROSPERITY IN ISRAEL'S HISTORY.

THIS WAS THE **GOLDEN AGE**.

SOLOMON SOON ESTABLISHED TRADING LINKS WITH HIS NEIGHBOURS, AND WITH HIS FATHER'S OLD ALLIES, BRINGING GREAT PROSPERITY TO ISRAEL.

KING HIRAM OF TYRE SENDS YOU THESE GIFTS, MY LORD, WITH HIS EVERY BLESSING.

BECAUSE OF THE WARS WAGED AGAINST MY FATHER FROM ALL SIDES HE COULD NOT BUILD A TEMPLE. BUT GOD HAS GIVEN US PEACE. LET'S USE IT TO HIS GLORY!

FOUR HUNDRED AND EIGHTY YEARS AFTER THE PEOPLE OF ISRAEL ESCAPED FROM EGYPT, THE CONSTRUCTION OF THE GREAT TEMPLE BEGAN.

THE LAND HAD BEEN SET ASIDE IN DAVID'S REIGN, ON ONE OF THE HILLS OF JERUSALEM – THE SAME PLACE WHERE ABRAHAM HAD MET GOD CENTURIES BEFORE.

THE MIGHTIEST TREES IN THE GREAT FORESTS OF LEBANON WERE FELLED FOR THEIR TIMBER, AND HAULED OVER LAND AND SEA TO JERUSALEM.

THE MEN WORKED IN NEAR SILENCE. THE STONE WAS CUT WHILE STILL IN THE QUARRIES, THE WOOD PLANED WHILE STILL IN THE FORESTS. A QUIET REVERENCE HUNG IN THE AIR.

IT WAS AS IF THE GROUND WAS HOLY FROM THE START.

A BUILDING NOT MEANT FOR PRIESTS OR KINGS, BUT A HOUSE FOR GOD.

AND SO, ALMOST 500 YEARS AFTER ITS MAKING, THE ARK WAS BROUGHT INTO THE TEMPLE.

... AND WAS FINALLY LAID TO REST.

THE ARK, CONTAINING THE STONE TABLETS GIVEN TO MOSES, WAS CARRIED INTO THE TEMPLE BY THE PRIESTS.

WORD OF SOLOMON'S FAME QUICKLY SPREAD THROUGHOUT THE KNOWN WORLD.

THE QUEEN OF **SHEBA**, A COUNTRY FAR TO THE SOUTH, HEARD OF SOLOMON, OF HIS FABULOUS PALACE AND INCREDIBLE WISDOM.

AND SO, BEARING WONDERFUL GIFTS, SHE MOUNTED A VAST EXPEDITION TO SEE THIS KING WITH HER OWN EYES.

PLEASE, ACCEPT THESE SPICES AS A TOKEN OF OUR GOODWILL.

YOUR COUNTRY MUST BE A **WONDERFUL** PLACE, SHEBA. I WOULD BE MORE THAN INTERESTED IN TRADE LINKS WITH YOU.

YOU DESIRE TO BE EVEN RICHER, THEN?

BUT YOU HAVE EVERYTHING YOU COULD EVER WANT.

EATING TOO MUCH HONEY WILL MAKE YOU **SICK**. IT'S THE SAME WITH MONEY. BUT IF YOU **HELP** OTHERS WITH WHAT YOU HAVE, THEN YOU'LL BE HELPED IN RETURN.

MORE **WEALTH**? NO – IT'S **FAR** BETTER TO BE POOR AND FEAR GOD THAN TO BE RICH AND LIVE A LIFE OF CONSTANT TROUBLE. IT'S **BETTER** TO ENJOY A SIMPLE BOWL OF COLD VEGETABLES WITH PEOPLE YOU LOVE, THAN TO GO TO A **BANQUET** WITH PEOPLE WHO COULDN'T CARE IF YOU LIVED OR DIED!

SOME WOULD SAY IT'S A SIGN OF WEAKNESS TO SHOW KINDNESS.

LET THEM. INSULTS CAN NEVER HURT YOU, UNLESS THEY'RE **TRUE**, OF COURSE.

IN THE END IT'S WHAT **YOU** SAY AND WHAT **YOU** DO THAT WILL AFFECT YOUR LIFE. IN THE END WE'LL ALL GET WHAT WE DESERVE, SO WHY NOT ALTER THE OUTCOME NOW?

YOU KNOW, EVERYTHING I HEARD ABOUT YOU IS TRUE. BUT I NEVER WOULD HAVE BELIEVED IT IF I HADN'T SEEN WITH MY OWN EYES.

YOUR GOD IS GOOD TO YOU! HE'S SHOWN HIS LOVE TO HIS PEOPLE BY MAKING YOU THEIR KING.

ISRAEL IS THE MOST BLESSED NATION IN THE WORLD.

SOLOMON WAS GREATER IN WISDOM AND WEALTH THAN ANY RULER ON EARTH. EVERY KING IN THE WORLD MADE HIS WAY TO ISRAEL TO ASK SOLOMON'S ADVICE.

ELIJAH HAD OBEYED GOD COMPLETELY IN GOING TO SEE THE KING, EVEN AT THE RISK OF HIS OWN LIFE.

BUT ELIJAH DIDN'T REJOICE. INSTEAD HE HID HIMSELF IN A RAVINE IN THE HILLS, AND FELL INTO A BLACK MOOD.

WHAT *NOW*, MY GOD?

I AM GOD. I WILL FEED YOU, ELIJAH.

GOD SENT *RAVENS* TO ELIJAH, AND THEY CARED FOR HIM.

EVERY MORNING AND EVERY EVENING THEY FLEW DOWN TO ELIJAH, AND BROUGHT HIM BREAD AND MEAT.

THERE WAS A TINY STREAM IN THE RAVINE, AND SO HE HAD WATER TO DRINK AS WELL AS THE FOOD THE BIRDS BROUGHT HIM.

AND SO ELIJAH SURVIVED, FED BY THE RAVENS AND DRINKING FROM THE SMALL STREAM, WHILE DROUGHT SAVAGED THE LAND AROUND HIM.

BUT EVENTUALLY THE STREAM DRIED UP.

SO GOD SENT ELIJAH NORTH, TO SEEK OUT A WIDOW AND HER SON.

GOOD DAY TO YOU! I WAS WONDERING IF YOU COULD SPARE ME SOME BREAD?

DON'T BE AFRAID. GO HOME AND MAKE YOUR MEAL, BUT BEFORE YOU DO, MAKE A SMALL LOAF FOR ME.

GOD SAYS IF YOU DO THIS, THE FLOUR AND OIL WILL NOT RUN OUT UNTIL HE SENDS *RAIN* AGAIN.

THE WOMAN DID AS ELIJAH SAID. EVERY TIME SHE EMPTIED THE JAR OF FLOUR, IT FILLED AGAIN, AND WHEN SHE USED UP THE LAST OF THE OIL, IT WAS REPLENISHED.

THE THREE OF THEM LIVED TOGETHER IN THE WIDOW'S HOUSE, PROTECTED AGAINST THE WORST OF THE FAMINE.

BREAD? WE HAVEN'T HAD BREAD FOR *WEEKS*! ALL I HAVE IS A TINY BIT OF FLOUR AND A DROP OF OIL.

I WAS GOING TO USE IT TO MAKE A CAKE. IT'S ALL WE HAVE LEFT, AND WHEN IT'S GONE WE'LL DIE!

ONE DAY ELIJAH MET *OBADIAH*, THE GOVERNOR OF KING AHAB'S PALACE, WHO HAD BEEN SENT IN SEARCH OF WATER. OBADIAH STILL LOVED AND SERVED GOD.

MY LORD ELIJAH, IS IT REALLY *YOU*?

YES, IT'S ME.

GO AND TELL THE KING WHERE I AM.

HEARD IT ALL BEFORE.

YES, BUT THE *RAIN*, REMEMBER THE TIME WHEN THE *DROUGHT* CAME..?

WHAT IF... WHAT IF HE'S *RIGHT*?

OH DON'T BE RIDICULOUS. HE'S JUST TRYING TO SCARE YOU, THAT'S ALL.

BUT WHAT IF HE'S RIGHT!?

WHAT DO YOU MEAN, 'IF'? COME ON ELISHA, WE MUST LEAVE.

GOD HAS SEEN WHAT WE'VE DONE! WE'RE *DOOMED*!

PLEASE MY LORD, EAT SOMETHING.

WOE TO ME! WOE TO US! WE'RE DOOMED!

REALLY, DARLING. DON'T GO ON! WE'VE NOTHING TO FEAR.

YOU DON'T *SEE* IT, DO YOU?

BECAUSE OF THE THINGS WE'VE DONE, THINGS YOU *MADE* ME DO, GOD WILL STICK TO HIS WORD!

I *KNOW* HE WILL!

BECAUSE HE REPENTED, GOD ALLOWED AHAB TO LIVE LONGER, BUT IT WAS ONLY A PUNISHMENT DEFERRED.

HE WENT TO WAR DISGUISED AS A COMMON SOLDIER LURKING AT THE REAR OF THE BATTLE, BUT A STRAY ARROW FOUND ITS MARK.

IT WAS A SLOW, PAINFUL END, AS HE LAY PROPPED AGAINST HIS CHARIOT, BLEEDING TO DEATH.

LATER THAT EVENING, DOGS CAME AND LICKED THE BLOOD FROM THE CHARIOT, AS ELIJAH HAD SAID THEY WOULD.

132

THE FALL OF ISRAEL AND JUDAH

AS THE NATIONS OF JUDAH AND ISRAEL SANK FURTHER INTO DEGENERACY SO GOD WITHDREW HIS PROTECTION. JERUSALEM WAS ATTACKED AGAIN AND AGAIN.

THROUGHOUT THESE TROUBLED TIMES THE EVENTS WERE RECORDED BY THOSE WHO REMAINED FAITHFUL TO GOD.

THE ENEMY HAS BREACHED THE SOUTH GATE! IT WON'T BE LONG NOW. IT'S HARD ENOUGH TRYING TO GET THIS ALL DOWN CORRECTLY, WITHOUT A *WAR* GOING ON!

ASSUMING I LIVE LONG ENOUGH TO FINISH IT; ASSUMING THERE'S ANYONE LEFT ALIVE TO *READ* IT! WHERE WAS I? OH YES, KING *AHAB* AND HIS REVOLTING WIFE, *JEZEBEL*! BAD TO THE BONE, THE PAIR OF THEM.

AS ELIJAH HAD PREDICTED, JEZEBEL DIED A VIOLENT DEATH. HURLED OUT OF A CASTLE WINDOW, HER BODY WAS TRAMPLED BY HORSES AND EATEN BY DOGS UNTIL THERE WASN'T ENOUGH LEFT TO BURY.

ALTHOUGH AHAB AND JEZEBEL HAD BEEN EVIL TO THE CORE, NONE OF THEIR SUCCESSORS WAS ANY BETTER: THE WORSHIP OF BAAL CAME TO A TEMPORARY HALT IN BLOODY AND VIOLENT SLAUGHTER, BUT THE PEOPLE STILL BOWED DOWN TO GOLDEN CALVES.

YOUNG JOASH REMAINED HIDDEN AWAY WITHIN THE TEMPLE ITSELF FOR SIX YEARS, PROTECTED BY THE FAITHFUL PRIEST JEHOIADA.

GOD HAD PROMISED DAVID THAT ONE OF HIS DESCENDANTS WOULD RULE THE KINGDOM THAT HAS *NO END*, AND THAT GOD HIMSELF WOULD BE A FATHER TO HIM.

IN JUDAH, IN A VICIOUS ATTEMPT TO WIN POWER, QUEEN ATHALIAH DESTROYED THE ENTIRE ROYAL FAMILY. THE HOUSE OF DAVID WAS ALL BUT WIPED OUT: THE ONLY SURVIVOR WAS A BABY BOY, THE YOUNG PRINCE *JOASH* RESCUED BY THE WIFE OF ONE OF THE PRIESTS.

IN ANY EVENT, JEHOIADA KNEW HIS POLITICS AS WELL AS HIS SCRIPTURES, AND SAW HE HAD AN OPPORTUNITY TO SEIZE POWER BACK FROM THE EVIL QUEEN.

WHEN JOASH WAS SEVEN YEARS OLD JEHOIADA SUMMONED THE GENERALS AND COMMANDERS OF THE ARMY TO THE TEMPLE, AND THEN AS THEY WAITED IN WONDER, HE PRODUCED HIS SURPRISE GUEST!

LISTEN TO ME! TODAY I HAVE ARMED YOU WITH THE WEAPONS KEPT IN THE TEMPLE — THE WEAPONS THAT BELONGED TO KING DAVID! TODAY WE RESTORE HIS *HEIR* TO THE THRONE!

SURROUND THE NEW KING AND THE TEMPLE! SUMMON THE GUARDS WHO ARE OFF DUTY AND HAVE THEM JOIN US! TODAY WE CROWN THE KING OURSELVES!

LONG LIVE KING JOASH! LONG LIVE KING JOASH!

GOD PROTECT THE NEW KING!

AS A PLAN, IT WAS *BRILLIANT*! JOASH WAS PUT ON THE THRONE OF JUDAH WITH SCARCELY A DROP OF BLOOD SPILLED!

NO! THIS IS *TREASON*!

GUARDS! *GUARDS*! I WANT HIM *DEAD*!!

CROWNED BY THE PRIEST JEHOIADA, SURROUNDED BY ARMED GUARDS, THERE WAS NOTHING THE QUEEN COULD DO TO PREVENT IT!

BUT THE ENTIRE ARMY BACKED THE NEW KING. WHEN THE GUARDS FINALLY ANSWERED THE QUEEN'S CALL, IT WAS ONLY TO TAKE HER TO A PLACE OF *EXECUTION*.

JOASH WAS A RARITY. A GOOD KING, HE TORE DOWN THE ALTARS TO BAAL, AND RESTORED THE OLD WAYS, BRINGING THE PEOPLE BACK TO GOD.

HE REBUILT THE TEMPLE, AND ENDED CORRUPTION IN THE PRIESTHOOD. BUT AFTER JEHOIADA'S DEATH JOASH ALSO TURNED HIS BACK ON GOD, EVEN ORDERING THAT JEHOIADA'S SON, A PROPHET, BE STONED TO DEATH IN THE VERY TEMPLE JOASH HAD HELPED TO REBUILD.

THE KINGS OF ISRAEL COULD NOT TURN FROM THE DARKNESS, AND SO GOD WITHDREW HIS PROTECTION ALTOGETHER.

KING HOSHEA WAS *THE LAST KING OF ISRAEL*, THE LAST OF THE NORTHERN KINGS.

HE HAD REIGNED AS A PUPPET OF HIS ASSYRIAN MASTERS, AND WAS FINALLY CAUGHT OUT ATTEMPTING TO BETRAY THEM TO THE EGYPTIANS.

THE PEOPLE OF THE NORTHERN KINGDOM OF ISRAEL WERE MADE SLAVES BY THE KING OF ASSYRIA, AND WERE TAKEN AWAY IN EXILE.

NOW ONLY THE SOUTHERN KINGDOM OF *JUDAH* SURVIVED. OF THE TWELVE TRIBES OF JACOB, ONLY TWO NOW REMAINED FREE, AND WITH THEM THE HOPE FOR ALL ISRAEL.

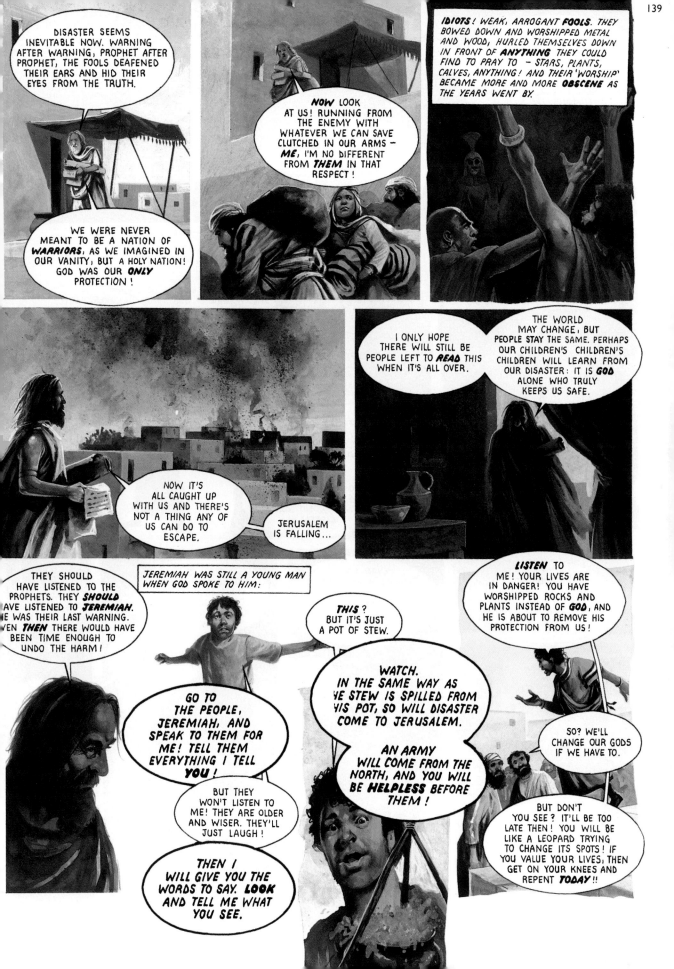

THEY DIDN'T LISTEN. THEY *NEVER* LISTENED. JEREMIAH SAW IT ALL, THOUGH. IT WAS AS IF HE COULD *HEAR* THE SOUNDS OF THE WOMEN CRYING FOR THEIR DEAD CHILDREN, AND *SMELL* THE BURNING CITY, AS IF IT WERE REAL.

HE WAS TORTURED BY THE VISIONS OF JERUSALEM, THE HOLY CITY OF GOD, TORN TO PIECES BY ITS OWN EVIL.

IN THE PLACES WHERE THEY HAD ONCE WORSHIPPED GOD, AND THE AIR HAD BEEN FULL OF SINGING AND LAUGHTER, THE PEOPLE *BURNED* THEIR OWN CHILDREN AS *SACRIFICES* TO STONES AND STARS AND TREES.

JEREMIAH WAS THROWN DOWN A WELL FOR HIS TROUBLE AND LEFT TO DIE.

HIS CONSTANT PREACHING WAS CONSIDERED BAD FOR MORALE.

LISTEN TO ME! IF WE STAY IN THE CITY WE WILL ALL *DIE*!

SURRENDER TO THE BABYLONIANS. GOD WILL BE MERCIFUL! WHY WON'T YOU *LISTEN*?!

YOUR MAJESTY, JEREMIAH WILL SURELY DIE IN THE WELL. THERE'S LITTLE ENOUGH FOOD IN THE CITY, LET ALONE WHERE HE IS. HE IS STILL A MAN OF GOD, AND DESERVES BETTER THAN THIS.

VERY WELL. BRING HIM UP TO THE COURTYARD, BUT HE'S NOT TO BE RELEASED. I DON'T WANT TO ANGER THE PEOPLE ANY FURTHER.

IT'S YOUR LUCKY DAY, TRAITOR. THE KING WANTS YOUR ADVICE, AND ASKS YOU TO TELL THE TRUTH.

IF I TELL THE TRUTH HE'LL HAVE ME KILLED, AND IF I GIVE HIM ADVICE HE WON'T LISTEN!

EVEN SO, JEREMIAH WAS SPARED. BUT HIS FATE WAS STILL TIED TO THE FATE OF THE PEOPLE BESIEGED IN THE CITY OF JERUSALEM AND...

WHAT'S THAT NOISE?

NO! NOT NOW! NOT WHEN I'VE ALMOST FINISHED!

EVEN IF MOSES AND SAMUEL STOOD HERE AND PLEADED, GOD WOULDN'T CHANGE HIS MIND NOW.

HEAR MY PRAYER, OH GOD, AND SHOW US MERCY.

DO NOT ABANDON YOUR PEOPLE FOR EVER, LORD MY GOD.

THE STORY OF JONAH

GOD SPOKE TO **JONAH**, A PROPHET OF ISRAEL, TELLING HIM TO GO TO THE CITY OF **NINEVEH**, AND TELL THE PEOPLE THERE TO SEEK FORGIVENESS FOR THEIR EVIL WAYS.

NINEVEH WAS ISRAEL'S HATED **ENEMY**, AND JONAH DIDN'T SEE **WHY** GOD SHOULD FORGIVE THEM. WHY COULDN'T HE JUST **DESTROY** THEM?

AND EVEN **THEN** HE DIDN'T STOP, BOARDING THE FIRST AVAILABLE SHIP BOUND FOR WHO-KNOWS-WHERE, JUST AS LONG AS IT WAS FAR, FAR AWAY FROM THE DOOMED CITY OF **NINEVEH**.

AND SO JONAH SET OFF AT ONCE, AS FAST AS HIS LEGS WOULD CARRY HIM - IN THE **OPPOSITE** DIRECTION!

IN FACT, JONAH KEPT ON RUNNING UNTIL HE REACHED THE **SEA**, AS FAR AWAY FROM NINEVEH AS HE COULD POSSIBLY GET.

OF COURSE, RUNNING AWAY FROM **PEOPLE** IS ONE THING - RUNNING AWAY FROM **GOD** IS A DIFFERENT MATTER ALTOGETHER.

THE SHIP WAS ONLY A FEW DAYS OUT OF PORT WHEN A TERRIBLE **STORM** TOOK HOLD, WORSE THAN ANYTHING THE CREW HAD EVER SEEN!

WE'RE TAKING IN WATER! ABANDON THE CARGO BEFORE WE GO UNDER!

IT'S NOT ENOUGH! WE'RE STILL OVERLADEN! WE'LL HAVE TO DRAW STRAWS AND THROW SOMEONE OVERBOARD!

IT'S ALL MY FAULT! **GOD** TOLD ME TO GO TO THE CITY OF MY ENEMIES, BUT I RAN AWAY INSTEAD!

BUT WE'RE ONLY GOING TO **SPAIN**! YOU CAN HIDE FROM GOD IN **SPAIN**!

I CAN SEE THAT **NOW**, OBVIOUSLY! LISTEN, IF YOU THROW ME OVERBOARD, THE STORM WILL STOP, I JUST **KNOW** IT WILL!

THIS ISN'T **YOUR** FAULT!

COME ON. LET'S GET IT OVER WITH.

I'VE JUST REMEMBERED! I CAN'T SWI-!

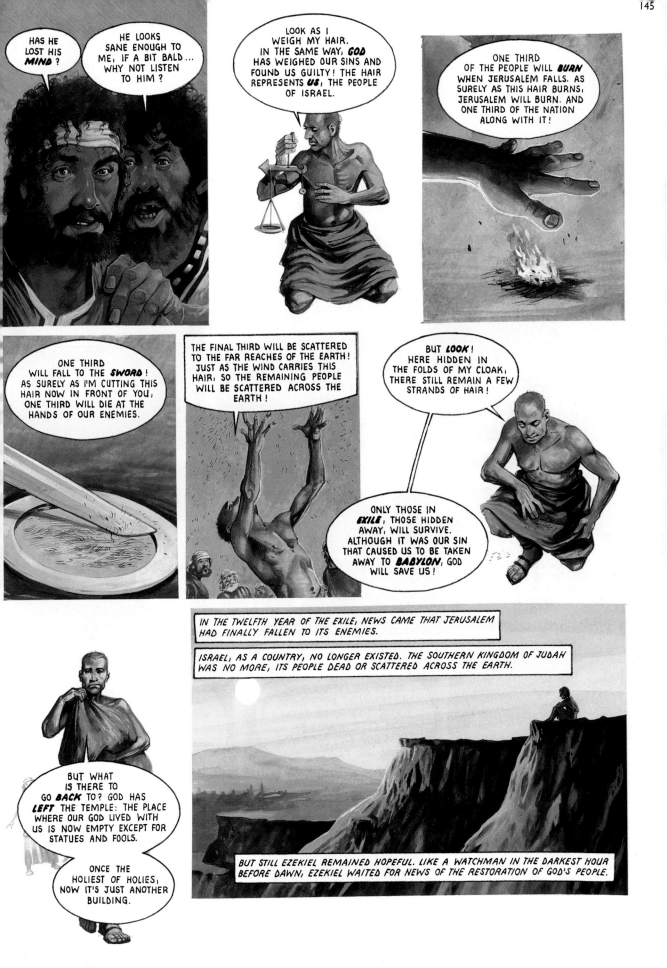

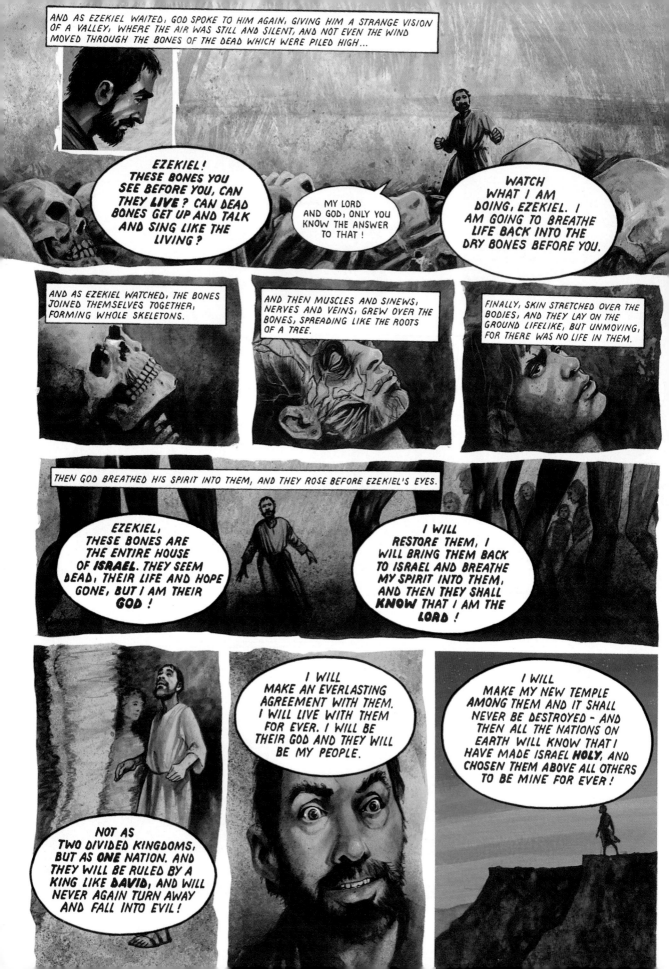

THE STORY OF DANIEL

NEBUCHADNEZZAR, THE KING OF BABYLONIA, TOOK A GREAT MANY ISRAELITES - OR JEWS AS THEY WERE ALSO KNOWN - AS PRISONERS, HAULING THEM OFF IN CHAINS TO HIS PALACE IN BABYLON.

HE WAS KING OF THE GREATEST NATION ON EARTH AND THERE WAS NO ONE WHO COULD RESIST HIM.

HE LOOTED THE TEMPLE AND TOOK THE GOLD AND SILVER TREASURES AS SPOILS OF WAR.

AMONG THE EXILES LIVING IN BABYLON WERE FOUR YOUNG MEN — SHADRACH, MESHACH AND ABEDNEGO, AND THEIR FRIEND **DANIEL** — WHO WERE SPECIALLY CHOSEN TO BE TRAINED TO BE ADVISORS AT THE ROYAL COURT. THE FOUR ISRAELITE STUDENTS RESISTED THE PRIVILEGES OF THE COURT AND KEPT TO THE LAWS OF THE TRUE GOD.

YOU'RE THE BRIGHTEST OF THE LOT, DANIEL. YOU INTERPRET MY DREAMS BETTER THAN ALL OF MY WISE MEN. YOU SHALL BE MY CHIEF ADVISER — YOUR GOD MUST BE VERY POWERFUL.

I CAN ONLY TELL YOU WHAT MY GOD HAS TOLD ME.

BUT NEBUCHADNEZZAR SOON FORGOT ABOUT DANIEL'S GOD AND BUILT A MASSIVE GOLD **STATUE**, INTENDING IT TO BE WORSHIPPED. HE CALLED THE OFFICIALS OF THE WHOLE KINGDOM TO COME TOGETHER FOR A CEREMONY OF DEDICATION.

WHY DO YOU NOT **KNEEL**?! HAVE I NOT ISSUED A **COMMAND**?

YOUR MAJESTY WE ARE **ISRAELITES**. WE ARE FORBIDDEN TO WORSHIP STATUES. WE CAN WORSHIP NO ONE BUT THE ONE TRUE GOD.

THEN LET **HIM** SAVE YOU, IF HE CAN!

GUARDS! TAKE THESE TRAITORS AND HAVE THEM THROWN INTO THE FURNACE! **BURN THEM ALIVE!**

JUDGES, LAWYERS, GOVERNORS, COMMISSIONERS, ALL CAME TO THE STATUE AND BOWED DOWN BEFORE IT. EVERYONE, THAT IS, EXCEPT THE **ISRAELITES** —

DANIEL'S THREE FRIENDS WERE TIED UP AND THROWN **ALIVE** INTO THE FURNACE; THE HEAT WAS SO FIERCE THAT THE GUARDS THEMSELVES WERE BADLY BURNED.

SEE? THERE ARE NO GODS WHO CAN **SAVE** YOU NOW!

YOU WERE WARNED BUT YOU WOULDN'T **LISTEN**! THERE ARE NO...

...! WHAT **IS** THIS? WHY ARE THERE **FOUR** MEN IN THERE?!

YOUR MAJESTY, WE ONLY THREW **THREE** MEN IN, I **SWEAR IT**!

THE FOURTH MAN IS DIFFERENT— HE LOOKS LIKE AN ANGEL OF GOD!

PRAISE THE GOD OF YOUR PEOPLE! YOU RISKED YOUR LIVES BY REFUSING TO WORSHIP ANY GOD BUT YOUR OWN! AND LOOK! THE ROPES HAVE BURNED AWAY, BUT YOU ARE UNHARMED! YOUR GOD HAS **SAVED** YOU!

FROM THIS DAY ON, IF **ANY** MAN SPEAKS ILL OF YOUR GOD, THEN I, THE **KING**, DECREE THAT HE BE TORN LIMB FROM LIMB!

HE ALONE IS GOD!

KING NEBUCHADNEZZAR DIED BELIEVING IN THE GOD OF ISRAEL, BUT HIS SON BELSHAZZAR NEITHER KNEW NOR CARED.

ONE NIGHT KING BELSHAZZAR THREW A PARTY FOR ALL THE NOBLES AND LORDS IN BABYLON.

THEY DRANK FROM THE VERY SAME GOLD CUPS THAT ONCE SAT IN THE TEMPLE IN **JERUSALEM**, NOW NO MORE THAN A **RUIN**. A FORGOTTEN, DEAD CITY IN A COUNTRY ON THE FAR SIDE OF THE CONTINENT.

HIS ONLY WEAKNESS IS HIS **RELIGION**! SURELY WE CAN USE IT TO SNARE HIM.

I'LL SUGGEST THE KING ISSUES A **DECREE** - NO ONE MAY ASK ANYTHING OF **ANY** GOD FOR A WHOLE MONTH! INSTEAD THEY SHOULD TAKE THEIR REQUESTS TO THE **KING**!

AND SO THE ORDER WAS PASSED. AS SOON AS DANIEL HEARD THE NEWS, HE WENT STRAIGHT TO HIS ROOM, STOOD IN FRONT OF HIS OPEN WINDOW —

AND **PRAYED**.

LOUDLY.

THE RESPONSE WAS IMMEDIATE. THE KING HAD GIVEN AN ORDER THAT COULD NOT BE REVOKED. DANIEL WOULD BE THROWN TO THE LIONS.

DANIEL! WHATEVER WERE YOU **THINKING**? PLEASE TELL ME YOU WERE SIMPLY **FORGETFUL**...

YOUR MAJESTY, I PRAYED AS I ALWAYS HAVE DONE. DELIBERATELY.

THEN MAY YOUR GOD SHOW YOU MERCY.

AND SO DANIEL WAS PUT IN A PIT WITH THE LIONS AND A HEAVY STONE WAS PUT OVER THE TOP.

THAT NIGHT, THE KING COULD NOT SLEEP. HE SENT HIS SERVANTS AWAY WHEN THEY BROUGHT FOOD AND ENTERTAINMENT.

GOVERNING THE KINGDOM WOULD BE ALL THE MORE DAUNTING WITHOUT DANIEL'S WISDOM AND COURAGE.

AT FIRST LIGHT, THE KING **RAN** TO THE LION PIT AND ORDERED THE GUARDS —

ROLL THE STONE AWAY AND BREAK THE SEALS ON THE CAGE! I NEED TO SEE FOR MYSELF!

DANIEL! WAS THE GOD YOU SERVE ABLE TO **SAVE** YOU?

152

THE STORY OF ESTHER

THROUGHOUT THE EXILE, THE JEWS CLUNG TO THE HOPE THAT ONE DAY THEY WOULD BE RETURNED TO ISRAEL.

IN THE LAND OF **PERSIA**, THE ISRAELITE EXILES FACED TERRIBLE DANGER, BUT ONE WOMAN'S COURAGE SAVED THE ENTIRE NATION FROM EXTERMINATION.

ESTHER WAS THE MOST BEAUTIFUL WOMAN IN THE PERSIAN KINGDOM. A JEWISH EXILE, SHE WAS MADE **QUEEN** OF PERSIA BY THE KING, XERXES.

NOW, ESTHER HAD A **COUSIN**, CALLED MORDECAI, WHO HAD CAUSE TO ARGUE WITH HAMAN, THE KING'S GOVERNOR.

MORDECAI, WHY DO YOU REFUSE TO KNEEL BEFORE ME? WHY DON'T YOU THANK OUR GODS THAT THEY HAVE SET ME UP AS THE KING'S GOVERNOR?

I AM A **JEW**, HAMAN. MY PEOPLE KNEEL ONLY BEFORE **GOD**.

THEN I WILL MAKE YOU **REGRET** YOUR FOOLISHNESS! THIS INSULT WILL NOT GO UNAVENGED!

EVEN SO, I STAND BY WHAT I HAVE SAID.

YOUR IMPERIAL MAJESTY, SOME OF THE FOREIGNERS ARE DISOBEYING YOUR WISHES, MOST EXALTED LORD AND MASTER.

AND WHAT DO YOU SUGGEST I DO?

DESTROY THEM. UTTERLY. EVERY LAST MAN, WOMAN AND CHILD – REMOVE THE TROUBLEMAKERS FOR EVER!

THE KING DID NOT KNOW THAT ESTHER WAS A **JEW**. HE ISSUED HIS ORDERS DECREEING DEATH TO ALL HER RACE A MONTH HENCE.

ESTHER, OF ALL THE PEOPLE IN PERSIA, ONLY **YOU** CAN SAVE US!

BUT I CAN'T APPROACH THE KING. ANYONE WHO GOES TO HIM WITHOUT BEING SUMMONED CAN BE PUT TO DEATH.

BUT DON'T YOU SEE? IF WE DIE, THEN GOD'S PLAN WILL COME TO **NOTHING**! PERHAPS IT WAS FOR THIS REASON THAT **YOU**, A JEW, WERE MADE QUEEN!

AND SO, TAKING HER LIFE IN HER HANDS, ESTHER APPROACHED THE KING, INVITING HIM TO A BANQUET, ALONG WITH HAMAN THE GOVERNOR.

SUCH INDEPENDENT THOUGHT MIGHT HAVE BEEN ENOUGH TO SIGN HER DEATH WARRANT, BUT SHE WAS SO BEAUTIFUL THE KING COULD REFUSE HER NOTHING!

THAT NIGHT AT THE BANQUET ESTHER GAVE THEM AN INVITATION TO ANOTHER BANQUET THE NEXT EVENING. SHE WOULD MAKE HER REQUEST THEN.

HAMAN WAS FLATTERED BY ALL THE ATTENTION.

A PLEASANT EVENING, HAMAN?

JEWISH DOG! I WAS HAVING A FINE EVENING UNTIL I SAW YOUR DISGUSTING FACE! AT LEAST I WON'T HAVE TO LOOK AT YOU FOR MUCH LONGER!

THE STORY OF EZRA AND NEHEMIAH

THE LONG YEARS OF EXILE ARE COMING TO AN END.

THE GREAT KINGDOM OF BABYLON HAS **FALLEN**, TO CYRUS, KING OF THE PERSIANS, WHO DECIDES TO RELEASE THE JEWS FROM THEIR EXILE.

AT LAST THEY CAN RETURN TO THE COUNTRY THEIR GRANDPARENTS SPOKE OF. FOR THE **SECOND** TIME IN THEIR HISTORY, THE JEWS MAKE THEIR WAY BACK TO ISRAEL, THE PROMISED LAND.

AND EVENTUALLY THEY ARRIVE IN **JERUSALEM**.

OVERGROWN, DERELICT AND SILENT, BUT FOR THE WILD ANIMALS WHO ROAM THE ONCE-BUSY STREETS. THE BROKEN WALLS LIE LIKE DRY BONES IN THE SUN...

IT'S AGREED THEN? WE START THE REBUILDING AT FIRST LIGHT. BUT THE TEMPLE **MUST** BE FIRST ON THE LIST.

AS SOON AS THE **FOUNDATIONS** ARE LAID WE CAN START OFFERING SACRIFICES AGAIN. WE'LL BUILD THE ROOF AND WALLS **AROUND** THE ALTAR IF WE HAVE TO!

AND SO THE WORK BEGAN - THE WRECKAGE OF THE OLD TEMPLE BEING RESHAPED INTO MATERIAL FOR THE NEW.

BUT ALMOST AS SOON AS THE REBUILDING STARTED, THE PROBLEMS BEGAN THAT WOULD PLAGUE THEM THROUGHOUT THEIR LABOURS.

THE NEIGHBOURING PEOPLES HAVE BEEN WATCHING US CLOSELY THESE PAST MONTHS. THEY WANT TO JOIN US IN REBUILDING THE TEMPLE. WHATEVER HAPPENS WE MUST **NEVER** ALLOW IT!

BUT WE COULD USE THEIR HELP!

WHILE WE WERE AWAY THEY'VE STARTED WORSHIPPING OTHER GODS. THEY WANT TO ADD THEIR GODS TO OURS IN THE TEMPLE, AND **THAT** WAS OUR DOWNFALL LAST TIME!

AGAINST THE ODDS THE TEMPLE WAS COMPLETED WITHIN 20 YEARS, BUT THE WALLS HAD TO WAIT...

BUT WHILE THE YOUNGER PEOPLE SHOUTED WITH **JOY** WITH EACH BRICK HIGHER THAN THE LAST, THE OLD PEOPLE, WHO COULD STILL JUST REMEMBER THE OLD JERUSALEM, COVERED THEIR HEADS AND WEPT WITH **SHAME**.

THE LOCAL PEOPLES DIDN'T TAKE KINDLY TO THE REBUTTAL, AND SOON THE BUILDERS FOUND THEMSELVES THE TARGET OF POLITICAL CONSPIRACIES, OF SLANDER, AND IN THE END, OF VIOLENCE ITSELF.

156

SOME SIXTY YEARS AFTER THE FIRST WAVE OF EXILES RETURNED, ANOTHER GROUP SET OUT ON THE LONG AND DANGEROUS JOURNEY BACK TO JERUSALEM, LED BY *EZRA*.

BY GOD'S GRACE I HAVE WON THE FAVOUR OF THE EMPEROR AND HIS COURT; THE LORD GOD HAS GIVEN ME COURAGE AND NOW... NOW WE CAN RETURN HOME.

BUT ON ARRIVAL IN JERUSALEM IT WAS CLEAR THAT DESPITE THE COMPLETION OF THE TEMPLE ALL WAS NOT WELL.

ISN'T THIS HOW OUR TROUBLES *STARTED*?

LORD GOD OF ISRAEL, YOU ARE JUST, BUT YOU HAVE LET US SURVIVE. WE CONFESS OUR GUILT TO YOU; WE HAVE NO RIGHT TO COME INTO YOUR PRESENCE.

GRIEF-STRICKEN AND FULL OF DESPAIR EZRA TORE HIS CLOTHES AND HAIR.

I CAN'T BELIEVE WHAT I'M HEARING! HOW CAN PEOPLE HAVE SUCH SHORT MEMORIES?! WE MUST FOLLOW GOD'S LAW AND THAT MEANS NO MARRIAGES OUTSIDE OUR COMMUNITY.

THERE IS NO *EASY* WAY TO SAY THIS! AND THIS IS NO *EASY* THING TO DO. BUT THOSE OF YOU WHO HAVE MARRIED OUTSIDE OUR COMMUNITY MUST SEPARATE YOURSELVES FROM YOUR WIVES IMMEDIATELY.

GOD HAS GIVEN US A SECOND CHANCE TO REBUILD OUR NATION, BUT IF WE DISOBEY HIM IT WILL COME TO NOTHING! WE ACCEPT THIS, OR WE ALL *PERISH*!

WHILE EZRA WEPT AND PRAYED A CROWD OF ISRAELITES GATHERED. TWO MEN CAME FORWARD. ONE OF THEM SPOKE ON BEHALF OF THE CROWD.

WE HAVE BROKEN FAITH WITH GOD. SHOW US HOW TO PURIFY OURSELVES. LEAD US, EZRA. INSTRUCT US AND WE *WILL* DO WHAT GOD'S LAW DEMANDS.

SO EZRA BEGAN HIS WORK. A MESSAGE WAS SENT THROUGHOUT JERUSALEM AND JUDAH THAT ALL THOSE WHO HAD RETURNED FROM EXILE WERE TO MEET IN THREE DAYS' TIME IN THE TEMPLE SQUARE.

THE CROWD KNEW THAT EZRA WAS RIGHT: THEY MUST FOLLOW GOD'S LAW OR FACE THE CONSEQUENCES.

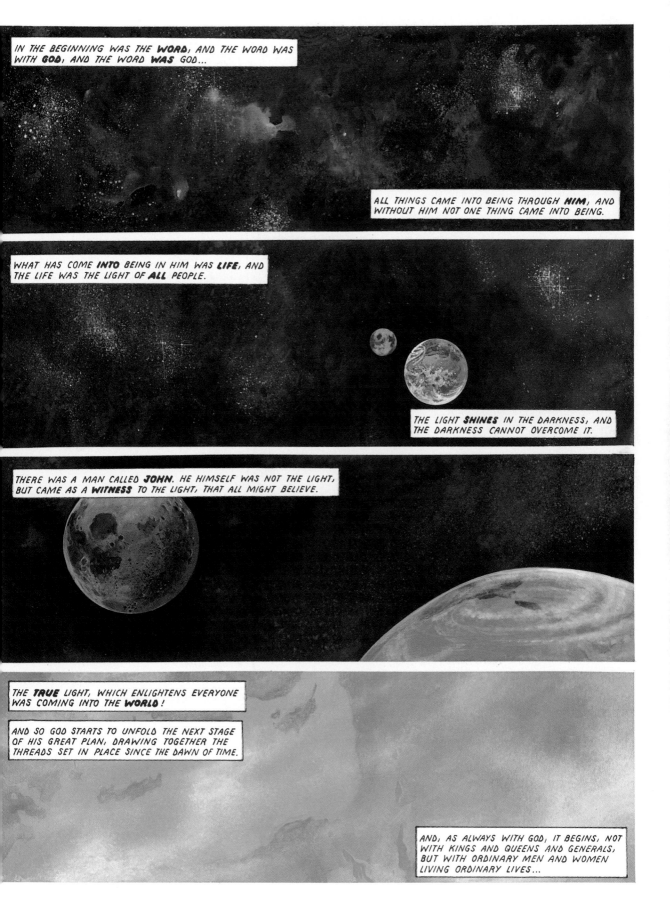

IN THE BEGINNING WAS THE **WORD**, AND THE WORD WAS WITH **GOD**, AND THE WORD **WAS** GOD...

ALL THINGS CAME INTO BEING THROUGH **HIM**, AND WITHOUT HIM NOT ONE THING CAME INTO BEING.

WHAT HAS COME **INTO** BEING IN HIM WAS **LIFE**, AND THE LIFE WAS THE LIGHT OF **ALL** PEOPLE.

THE LIGHT **SHINES** IN THE DARKNESS, AND THE DARKNESS CANNOT OVERCOME IT.

THERE WAS A MAN CALLED **JOHN**. HE HIMSELF WAS NOT THE LIGHT, BUT CAME AS A **WITNESS** TO THE LIGHT, THAT ALL MIGHT BELIEVE.

THE **TRUE** LIGHT, WHICH ENLIGHTENS EVERYONE WAS COMING INTO THE **WORLD**!

AND SO GOD STARTS TO UNFOLD THE NEXT STAGE OF HIS GREAT PLAN, DRAWING TOGETHER THE THREADS SET IN PLACE SINCE THE DAWN OF TIME.

AND, AS ALWAYS WITH GOD, IT BEGINS, NOT WITH KINGS AND QUEENS AND GENERALS, BUT WITH ORDINARY MEN AND WOMEN LIVING ORDINARY LIVES...

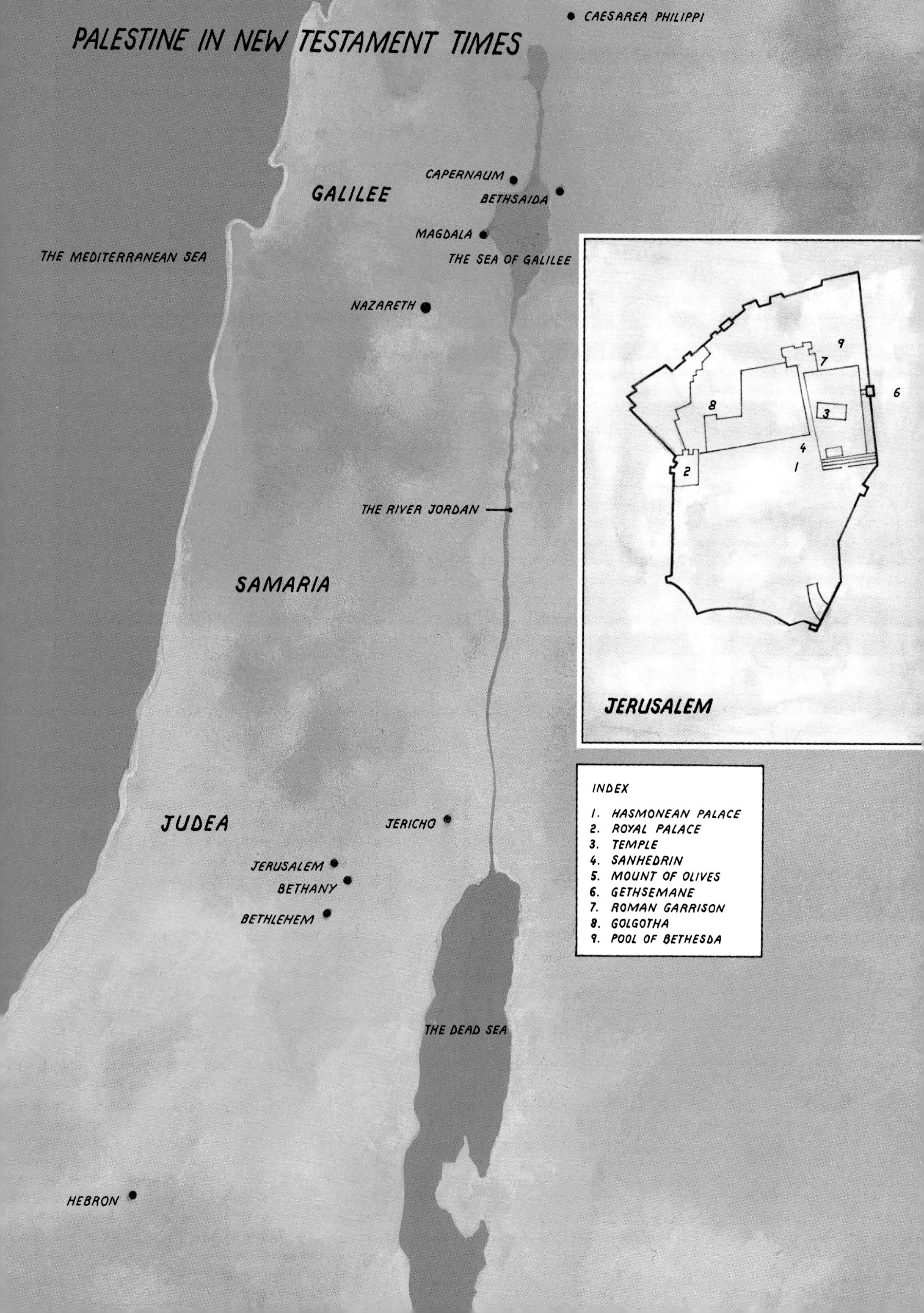

160

PALESTINE IN NEW TESTAMENT TIMES

● CAESAREA PHILIPPI

GALILEE

CAPERNAUM ●
BETHSAIDA ●
●
MAGDALA ●
THE SEA OF GALILEE

THE MEDITERRANEAN SEA

NAZARETH ●

THE RIVER JORDAN ⟶

SAMARIA

JUDEA

JERICHO ●

JERUSALEM ●
BETHANY ●
BETHLEHEM ●

THE DEAD SEA

HEBRON ●

JERUSALEM

INDEX

1. HASMONEAN PALACE
2. ROYAL PALACE
3. TEMPLE
4. SANHEDRIN
5. MOUNT OF OLIVES
6. GETHSEMANE
7. ROMAN GARRISON
8. GOLGOTHA
9. POOL OF BETHESDA

WHICH BRINGS US TO NAZARETH, A TOWN IN THE HILL-COUNTRY OF GALILEE, IN THE NORTH OF ISRAEL.

MARY, A YOUNG WOMAN, IS ENGAGED TO BE MARRIED TO JOSEPH, A LOCAL CARPENTER.

UNDER ROMAN OCCUPATION, ISRAEL IS RULED BY A PUPPET KING, CORRUPT, AND DIVORCED FROM THE PEOPLE.

BUT JOSEPH IS A DESCENDANT OF KING DAVID, IN A LINE THAT STRETCHES BACK TO ABRAHAM.

HERE, THROUGH THE LIVES OF ORDINARY PEOPLE, AMIDST THE UNREMARKABLE AND THE MUNDANE, GOD FINALLY BRINGS HIS PLAN TO FRUITION.

SOMETHING WONDERFUL IS ABOUT TO HAPPEN...

REJOICE, MARY, FOR GOD IS WITH YOU! BLESSED ARE YOU AMONG WOMEN! OF ALL THE WOMEN ON EARTH, YOU HAVE FOUND FAVOUR WITH GOD!

BE AT PEACE, AND HAVE NO FEAR!

ME? BUT I DON'T UNDERSTAND — I MEAN, I'M NO ONE SPECIAL. WHAT HAVE I DONE?

YOU WILL HAVE A CHILD, AND HIS NAME WILL BE JESUS!

HE WILL BE CALLED THE SON OF THE MOST HIGH. THE LORD GOD HIMSELF WILL GIVE HIM THE THRONE OF HIS ANCESTOR, DAVID. HE WILL RULE THE DESCENDANTS OF THE HOUSE OF JACOB FOR EVER!

AND OF HIS KINGDOM, THERE WILL BE NO END!

BUT HOW? I'M NOT PREGNANT; I'M NOT EVEN MARRIED, I — I'M STILL A VIRGIN!

THE HOLY SPIRIT WILL REST UPON YOU, AND THE POWER OF GOD WILL OVERSHADOW YOU. IN THIS WAY YOUR CHILD WILL BE CALLED THE SON OF GOD.

NOTHING IS IMPOSSIBLE TO GOD! YOUR OWN RELATIVE, ELIZABETH — CHILDLESS AND PAST CHILD-BEARING — IS NOW SIX MONTHS PREGNANT. NOTHING IS IMPOSSIBLE, MARY! NOTHING!

STIRRED BY THE ANGEL'S WORDS, MARY MADE HER WAY SOUTH TO THE HILLS OF JUDEA, TO VISIT HER COUSIN ELIZABETH. PERHAPS SHE COULD ANSWER SOME OF MARY'S QUESTIONS.

BUT ELIZABETH'S GREETING TOOK HER ABACK...

MARY! GOD'S BLESSING IS ON YOU ABOVE ALL WOMEN ON EARTH, AND BLESSED IS THE CHILD YOU WILL BEAR!

AS SOON AS I HEARD YOUR VOICE, THE CHILD IN MY WOMB LEAPED FOR JOY!!

MY SPIRIT AND MY SOUL REJOICE IN GOD. FROM THIS DAY ON, ALL PEOPLE WILL COUNT ME HAPPY, BECAUSE OF WHAT GOD HAS DONE. HE HAS KEPT HIS PROMISE TO COME TO HIS PEOPLE'S AID.

MARY STAYED THREE MONTHS WITH HER COUSIN, AND THEN RETURNED HOME.

163

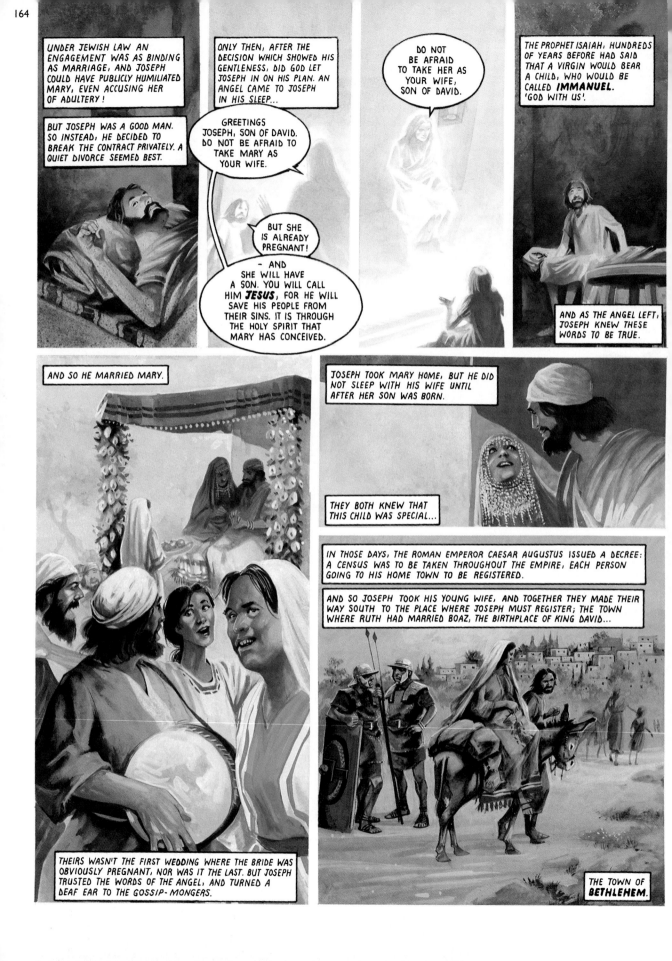

UNDER JEWISH LAW AN ENGAGEMENT WAS AS BINDING AS MARRIAGE, AND JOSEPH COULD HAVE PUBLICLY HUMILIATED MARY, EVEN ACCUSING HER OF ADULTERY!

BUT JOSEPH WAS A GOOD MAN. SO INSTEAD, HE DECIDED TO BREAK THE CONTRACT PRIVATELY. A QUIET DIVORCE SEEMED BEST.

ONLY THEN, AFTER THE DECISION WHICH SHOWED HIS GENTLENESS, DID GOD LET JOSEPH IN ON HIS PLAN. AN ANGEL CAME TO JOSEPH IN HIS SLEEP...

GREETINGS JOSEPH, SON OF DAVID. DO NOT BE AFRAID TO TAKE MARY AS YOUR WIFE.

BUT SHE IS ALREADY PREGNANT!

- AND SHE WILL HAVE A SON. YOU WILL CALL HIM *JESUS*, FOR HE WILL SAVE HIS PEOPLE FROM THEIR SINS. IT IS THROUGH THE HOLY SPIRIT THAT MARY HAS CONCEIVED.

DO NOT BE AFRAID TO TAKE HER AS YOUR WIFE, SON OF DAVID.

THE PROPHET ISAIAH, HUNDREDS OF YEARS BEFORE HAD SAID THAT A VIRGIN WOULD BEAR A CHILD, WHO WOULD BE CALLED *IMMANUEL*. 'GOD WITH US'.

AND AS THE ANGEL LEFT, JOSEPH KNEW THESE WORDS TO BE TRUE.

AND SO HE MARRIED MARY.

THEIRS WASN'T THE FIRST WEDDING WHERE THE BRIDE WAS OBVIOUSLY PREGNANT, NOR WAS IT THE LAST. BUT JOSEPH TRUSTED THE WORDS OF THE ANGEL, AND TURNED A DEAF EAR TO THE GOSSIP-MONGERS.

JOSEPH TOOK MARY HOME, BUT HE DID NOT SLEEP WITH HIS WIFE UNTIL AFTER HER SON WAS BORN.

THEY BOTH KNEW THAT THIS CHILD WAS SPECIAL...

IN THOSE DAYS, THE ROMAN EMPEROR CAESAR AUGUSTUS ISSUED A DECREE: A CENSUS WAS TO BE TAKEN THROUGHOUT THE EMPIRE, EACH PERSON GOING TO HIS HOME TOWN TO BE REGISTERED.

AND SO JOSEPH TOOK HIS YOUNG WIFE, AND TOGETHER THEY MADE THEIR WAY SOUTH TO THE PLACE WHERE JOSEPH MUST REGISTER; THE TOWN WHERE RUTH HAD MARRIED BOAZ, THE BIRTHPLACE OF KING DAVID...

THE TOWN OF **BETHLEHEM**.

IMMEDIATELY AFTER HE WAS BAPTIZED, THE SPIRIT TOOK JESUS FAR OUT INTO THE DESERT.

THERE, WITHOUT FOOD, HE STAYED FOR FORTY DAYS AND NIGHTS.

HE BURNED BY DAY...

AND HE FROZE BY NIGHT.

ALONE, AND FAR FROM FRIENDS, JESUS ENCOUNTERED THE **DEVIL**.

AND THEN, WHEN HE WAS AT HIS WEAKEST AND MOST VULNERABLE, HIS TRIALS BEGAN IN EARNEST.

WHO TRIED TO **TEMPT** HIM...

I AM SO HUNGRY. LORD GOD, PLEASE HELP ME WITH THIS HUNGER. THE PAIN IS TOO MUCH...

YOU? **HUNGRY**? WHY, JESUS, IF YOU'RE THE SON OF GOD, WHY DON'T YOU COMMAND THE STONES TO BECOME BREAD?

YOU KNOW THEY WILL. YOU KNOW HOW **GOOD** THEY'LL TASTE.

DO IT. DO IT **NOW**!

IT IS WRITTEN: 'MAN DOESN'T LIVE ON BREAD ALONE, BUT BY THE WORDS THAT COME FROM GOD'S MOUTH.' THEREFORE I WON'T USE GOD'S POWER FOR MY OWN NEEDS.

THEN *LOOK.* I WILL GIVE YOU ALL THE KINGDOMS ON EARTH, IF YOU WILL BOW DOWN AND WORSHIP *ME* !

IT IS WRITTEN: 'WORSHIP ONLY GOD, AND SERVE ONLY *HIM* !'

IF YOU *ARE* THE SON OF GOD, WHY NOT THROW YOURSELF FROM THE HIGHEST ROOF OF THE TEMPLE? SURELY GOD WILL SAVE YOU.

YOU COULD DO ANYTHING YOU *WISHED* AND GOD WOULD SAVE YOU! WHY NOT *DO* IT ?

IT IS WRITTEN: 'DO NOT PUT THE LORD YOUR GOD TO THE TEST.'

LEAVE ME, SATAN. I WILL NOT TURN FROM GOD.

AND AS THE DEVIL LEFT, *ANGELS* CAME, AND TENDED TO JESUS IN THE DESERT.

HE HAD NOT GIVEN IN AS *ADAM* HAD. JESUS' WORK ON EARTH COULD BEGIN...

JESUS BEGAN TO SEARCH FOR PEOPLE TO HELP HIM IN HIS WORK.

THE FIRST CHOSEN WERE A GROUP OF FISHERMEN, WORKING THE SHORES OF LAKE GALILEE.

ANDREW! PETER !

FOLLOW ME !

AND AT ONCE THE BROTHERS LEFT THEIR NETS AND FOLLOWED JESUS.

AND SO JESUS BEGAN TO TEACH. AND AS HE SPOKE, PEOPLE FLOCKED TO LISTEN IN THEIR *HUNDREDS*.

HE WAS UNLIKE ANYONE THEY HAD EVER HEARD BEFORE...

BLESSED ARE YOU WHO ARE *POOR*. FOR YOURS IS THE KINGDOM OF GOD. BLESSED ARE YOU WHO ARE *HUNGRY* AND WEEP, FOR YOU WILL BE FED AND SHED TEARS OF JOY!

BLESSED ARE YOU WHO ARE *PEACEMAKERS*, FOR YOU WILL BE GOD'S OWN CHILDREN.

I TELL YOU NOW, *LOVE* YOUR ENEMIES. SHOW KINDNESS TO THOSE WHO HATE YOU. TREAT OTHERS IN THE WAY *YOU* WANT TO BE TREATED.

IF SOMEONE STRIKES YOU ON ONE SIDE OF YOUR FACE, SAY 'HERE, HIT THE OTHER SIDE TOO!'

IF YOU CATCH SOMEONE STEALING YOUR CLOAK, THEN SAY 'HERE, HAVE MY TUNIC AS WELL!'

IF YOU'RE ONLY KIND TO THE PEOPLE WHO ARE KIND TO *YOU*, WHAT'S THE GOOD OF THAT? EVEN MURDERERS TREAT THEIR FRIENDS WELL.

DON'T JUDGE PEOPLE, AND *YOU* WON'T BE JUDGED. *FORGIVE* PEOPLE, AND *YOU* WILL BE FORGIVEN.

IF YOU SHOW KINDNESS TO OTHERS, DO IT *QUIETLY*. DON'T ANNOUNCE YOUR GOOD DEEDS WITH *TRUMPETS* LIKE THE HYPOCRITES.

GOD SEES EVERYTHING.

HIS REPUTATION AS A HEALER AND TEACHER GREW...

IS SHE ILL, PETER?

DYING. SHE'S BURNING WITH FEVER - I DON'T THINK SHE WILL LAST THE NIGHT.

MASTER! THANK YOU FOR COMING! IT'S MY WIFE'S MOTHER. I DON'T KNOW WHAT'S WRONG WITH HER.

I SEE.

THERE. HOW DO YOU FEEL?

OH! I FEEL - I FEEL WONDERFUL!

JESUS TOUCHED THE WOMAN'S HAND AND THE FEVER LEFT HER.

MY! SO MANY GUESTS IN THE HOUSE!

NOW THEN, WHO'S HUNGRY AND WANTS TO JOIN ME IN SOMETHING TO EAT? I'M STARVING!

JESUS STAYED UP ALL THAT NIGHT, HEALING ANYONE WHO WOULD COME TO HIM.

FROM MILES AROUND, PEOPLE BROUGHT THE SICK AND SUFFERING, AND JESUS HEALED THEM ALL.

YOUR GRANDSON WILL BE FINE NOW, BUT YOU MUST TELL NO ONE WHAT HAPPENED HERE TONIGHT.

THEN WHAT THE PEOPLE SAY MUST BE TRUE - YOU ARE THE SON OF GOD!

AGAIN, I TELL YOU, TELL NO ONE ABOUT THIS!

THE JEWS WERE WAITING FOR THE MESSIAH TO OVERTHROW THE ROMANS. JESUS KNEW GOD HAD OTHER PLANS...

NEAR THE SHORES OF THE LAKE THEY WERE MET BY A ROMAN OFFICIAL, SENT BY THE CENTURION OF THE NEARBY GARRISON.

THE CENTURION HAD A SERVANT WHO WAS SICK, AND JESUS HAD BEEN ASKED TO HEAL HIM.

MY MASTER SAYS NOT TO CONCERN YOURSELF WITH MAKING THE JOURNEY TO VISIT US.

WHY NOT? IS THE SICK MAN *WELL* AGAIN?

NO SIR, HE IS *DYING*. BUT MY MASTER GIVES THIS MESSAGE:

'IF YOU SIMPLY SAY THE WORD, MY SERVANT WILL BE HEALED. I TOO AM A MAN UNDER AUTHORITY. IF I TELL A SOLDIER "DO THIS", I KNOW IT WILL BE DONE. I SEE THAT SAME AUTHORITY IN YOU.'

SUCH *FAITH*...

I HAVE NEVER SEEN SUCH FAITH IN ALL OF *ISRAEL*; AND YET HERE IT IS COMING FROM A *ROMAN*...

GO HOME. THE MAN *WILL* BE HEALED JUST AS YOU SAID.

MASTER, I'VE DECIDED TO *FOLLOW* YOU, BUT FIRST LET ME SAY GOODBYE TO MY FAMILY.

NO ONE WHO PUTS A HAND TO THE PLOUGH AND LOOKS BACK IS FIT FOR THE KINGDOM OF GOD.

JESUS DID NOT WANT THE JEWS TO KNOW HIS TRUE IDENTITY, UNTIL THE TIME WAS RIGHT. AS HEIR TO KING DAVID, MANY EXPECTED HIM TO BE *LIKE* KING DAVID - A SOLDIER, LEADING A GREAT ARMY.

THE *ZEALOTS*, A GROUP OF FREEDOM FIGHTERS, WERE PLANNING TO OVERTHROW THE ROMANS AT ANY MOMENT, AND NEWS OF THE MESSIAH WOULD BE THE SPARK THEY NEEDED TO IGNITE THE REBELLION.

182

MORE AND MORE PEOPLE CAME TO SEE JESUS, ASKING HIM TO HEAL THEIR SICK.

MASTER, A MAN CALLED JAIRUS, THE LEADER OF THE LOCAL SYNAGOGUE, ASKS FOR YOU.

MY LITTLE DAUGHTER IS DYING! PLEASE, SHE IS ALL WE HAVE IN THE WORLD. IF YOU PUT YOUR HANDS ON HER I KNOW SHE WILL *LIVE*!

THE DISCIPLES SOON HAD THEIR HANDS FULL CONTROLLING THE CROWDS.

AMONG THE CROWD WAS A WOMAN, WHO HAD SUFFERED FROM CONSTANT BLEEDING FOR YEARS. NO DOCTOR COULD HELP HER. BUT SHE THOUGHT – 'IF ONLY I COULD TOUCH JESUS' CLOAK I WOULD BE WELL AGAIN.'

AND AS SHE BRUSHED HIS CLOAK WITH HER FINGERTIPS –

EVENTUALLY SHE REACHED JESUS...

–SHE WAS *HEALED*.

WHO *TOUCHED* ME?

SOMEONE TOUCHED MY CLOAK. I FELT POWER GO OUT FROM ME.

THE WOMAN, WHO WAS FULL OF FEAR, TOLD JESUS EVERYTHING.

DAUGHTER, YOUR FAITH HAS HEALED YOU.

GO IN PEACE, AND KNOW THAT YOU ARE FREE FROM YOUR SUFFERING.

JOHN THE BAPTIST HAD SPOKEN OUT AGAINST KING HEROD ANTIPAS, SON OF THE KING WHO HAD ORDERED THE SLAUGHTER OF INNOCENT CHILDREN SOON AFTER JESUS WAS BORN.

JOHN HAD PUBLICLY DENOUNCED THE KING FOR MARRYING HIS BROTHER'S WIFE, HERODIAS, AS THIS WAS AGAINST THE LAW OF MOSES. JOHN WAS DRAGGED OFF TO PRISON THE SAME DAY.

WHILE THE KING DECIDED WHAT TO DO WITH JOHN, HE THREW A PARTY TO CELEBRATE HIS **BIRTHDAY.**

THE MAIN ATTRACTION AT THE PARTY WAS HERODIAS'S DAUGHTER, SALOME, WHO DANCED FOR HEROD AND HIS GUESTS.

ASK ANYTHING OF ME, AND IT SHALL BE YOURS!

ANYTHING?

NAME IT!

VERY WELL.

HEROD WAS SO PLEASED WITH SALOME THAT HE MADE A RASH PROMISE TO HER, IN FRONT OF HIS ENTIRE COURT...

GIVE ME THE HEAD OF JOHN THE BAPTIST, HACKED OFF AND ON A SILVER PLATE.

THERE WAS NO WAY HEROD COULD BACK DOWN IN FRONT OF SO MANY IMPORTANT PEOPLE.

DO AS SHE SAYS.

HAVE JOHN BEHEADED AND HIS HEAD SERVED ON A SILVER PLATE. HIS DISCIPLES MAY HAVE THE REST OF THE BODY TO BURY AS THEY SEE FIT.

AND BESIDES, HIS WIFE HAD PUT THE GIRL UP TO IT, HE WAS SURE. HERODIAS **HATED** JOHN.

ONE DAY, AS JESUS WALKED ALONG THE SHORES OF LAKE GALILEE, THE CROWDS BECAME SO LARGE HE HAD TO STAND IN A FISHERMAN'S BOAT TO MAKE HIMSELF HEARD.

THE KINGDOM OF GOD IS LIKE THIS:

THERE WAS ONCE A FARMER WHO WENT TO SOW SEED. AS HE SCATTERED THE SEED, SOME FELL ON THE PATH AND BIRDS CAME AND ATE IT UP STRAIGHT AWAY.

'OTHER SEED FELL AMONG THORNS, WHICH CHOKED THE PLANTS BEFORE THEY HAD A CHANCE TO GROW PROPERLY.

'THE SEED IS GOD'S MESSAGE. SOME PEOPLE IGNORE IT; SOME TAKE TO IT AT ONCE, BUT IT NEVER TAKES ROOT. OTHERS BELIEVE FOR A WHILE, BUT LIFE'S WORRIES CROWD IN AND THEY FALL AWAY; BUT OTHERS ALLOW IT TO GROW IN THEIR LIVES AND FLOURISH.'

'SOME SEED FELL ON ROCKY GROUND AND SPRANG UP IN THE THIN SOIL. WHEN THE SUN CAME UP THE PLANTS WITHERED AWAY.

'BUT OTHER SEED FELL ON THE **GOOD** SOIL, WHERE IT PRODUCED A FINE CROP, MANY TIMES OVER.

THE KINGDOM OF HEAVEN IS LIKE THIS: ONCE UPON A TIME A MAN WAS DIGGING IN A FIELD WHEN HE STRUCK A HARD OBJECT...

'THE FIELD WOULD COST ALL HE HAD, SO HE SOLD EVERYTHING TO RAISE ENOUGH MONEY. THE MAN WAS FULL OF JOY FOR THE TREASURE WOULD BE HIS.'

'HE DUG UP A GOLD JAR FULL OF TREASURE – RINGS AND GOLD COINS. IF HE COULD BUY THE FIELDS HE WOULD RIGHTLY OWN THE TREASURE.

LATER, JESUS WAS DINING AT THE HOUSE OF A PHARISEE AND TOLD ANOTHER STORY ABOUT THE KINGDOM OF HEAVEN.

A MAN ONCE THREW A FABULOUS FEAST, A WONDERFUL BANQUET FOR ALL HIS FRIENDS.

'BUT THEY WERE SO SPOILT AND UNGRATEFUL THAT ON THE DAY OF THE FEAST THEY ALL MADE EXCUSES AND DIDN'T COME.

'SO THE MAN SENT HIS SERVANT OUT ONTO THE STREETS TO CALL THE HOMELESS, THE BEGGARS, LEPERS AND CRIPPLES, AND INVITED **THEM** TO HIS HOME FOR THE FEAST.

'THE MAN SAID: "NOT ONE OF THE GUESTS I FIRST INVITED WILL GET EVEN A **TASTE** OF MY BANQUET."'

198

SOME DAYS LATER, JESUS TOOK PETER, JAMES AND JOHN, AND LED THEM UP A NEARBY MOUNTAIN.

ON THE SUMMIT, JESUS BEGAN TO PRAY.

HIS THREE COMPANIONS, EXHAUSTED BY THE CLIMB, HAD OTHER IDEAS.

BUT AS JESUS PRAYED, AN INCREDIBLE *CHANGE* CAME OVER HIM... ONE THE DISCIPLES COULDN'T HELP BUT NOTICE.

... MASTER?

JESUS STOOD BEFORE THEM, HIS FACE SHINING LIKE THE *SUN*, HIS CLOTHES AS BRIGHT AS DAYLIGHT! IT HURT THEIR EYES EVEN TO *LOOK* AT HIM.

ON ONE SIDE OF JESUS STOOD MOSES AND ON THE OTHER THE PROPHET ELIJAH.

THE THREE FIGURES TALKED ABOUT THE WAY THAT GOD WOULD SOON FULFIL HIS PLAN, THROUGH JESUS' DEATH IN JERUSALEM.

MASTER! WHAT CAN I DO? LET ME MAKE THREE SHELTERS, ONE FOR EACH OF YOU!

PETER DIDN'T KNOW WHAT HE WAS SAYING, HE WAS SO OVERCOME WITH SHEER WONDER.

JUST THEN A CLOUD COVERED THE MOUNTAIN, AND A VOICE CAME FROM IT, SAYING:

THIS IS MY *SON* WHOM I LOVE. *LISTEN* TO HIM!

THE DISCIPLES FOLLOWED JESUS BACK DOWN THE MOUNTAIN IN SILENCE.

THEY HAD WITNESSED SOMETHING OF SUCH *ENORMITY*, THAT IT WOULD BE A LONG WHILE BEFORE THEY COULD FIND THE WORDS TO EVEN *BEGIN* TO DESCRIBE IT.

THE RAISING OF LAZARUS LED MANY JEWS TO PUT THEIR FAITH IN JESUS. FROM THAT MOMENT ON, THE CHIEF PRIESTS IN JERUSALEM MADE PLANS TO HAVE JESUS KILLED.

AND NOT JUST JESUS, BUT LAZARUS TOO — A WALKING REMINDER OF JESUS' POWER.

ALTHOUGH JESUS KNEW ALL OF THIS, HE LED HIS DISCIPLES TO THE CITY OF *JERUSALEM.*

IT WAS THE TIME OF THE PASSOVER.

AND SO THE DISCIPLES DID AS HE SAID, TELLING THE OWNER, 'THE MASTER NEEDS HIM,' JUST AS JESUS HAD TOLD THEM.

YOU TWO, GO TO THE VILLAGE AHEAD. YOU'LL FIND A DONKEY THERE THAT HAS NEVER BEEN RIDDEN. BRING HIM TO ME.

CENTURIES BEFORE, THE PROPHET ZECHARIAH HAD FORETOLD THESE EVENTS:

'REJOICE, YOU PEOPLE OF JERUSALEM.

'LOOK, YOUR KING HAS COME TO YOU! HE COMES VICTORIOUS, BUT ALSO HUMBLE, RIDING A YOUNG DONKEY.

'HE WILL MAKE *PEACE* BETWEEN THE NATIONS AND RULE FROM SEA TO SEA TO THE ENDS OF THE EARTH.'

THE GREAT CROWD THAT HAD COME TO JERUSALEM FOR THE PASSOVER HEARD THAT JESUS WAS COMING. AS HE ENTERED THE CITY, SHOUTS AND CHEERS FILLED THE AIR: '*HOSANNA! THE PROMISED KING HAS COME!* BLESSED IS HE WHO COMES IN THE NAME OF THE LORD.'

PEOPLE TOOK OFF THEIR CLOAKS AND LAID THEM IN JESUS' PATH. OTHERS LAID PALM LEAVES ON THE GROUND IN FRONT OF HIM.

IT WAS AS IF KING DAVID HIMSELF HAD RETURNED, TO RESTORE ISRAEL TO ITS FORMER GLORY.

THIS BREAD — TAKE AND EAT; THIS IS MY BODY, GIVEN FOR YOU. DO THIS IN REMEMBRANCE OF ME.

TAKE THIS CUP — DRINK FROM IT, ALL OF YOU. THIS IS MY BLOOD, POURED OUT FOR MANY FOR THE FORGIVENESS OF SINS.

'I TELL YOU THE TRUTH — I WILL NOT DRINK THE FRUIT OF THE VINE AGAIN, UNTIL THE KINGDOM OF GOD COMES.'

WHEN THEY HAD FINISHED THEIR MEAL, JESUS AND HIS DISCIPLES WENT OUTSIDE THE CITY WALLS — TO THE MOUNT OF OLIVES — TO PRAY.

WHIPPED, BEATEN, BLEEDING AND COVERED IN SPIT, THE HEIR TO THE THRONE OF DAVID WAS FINALLY CROWNED *KING*. THEN THEY LED HIM AWAY TO CRUCIFY HIM.

ALL AUTHORITY IN HEAVEN AND EARTH HAS BEEN GIVEN TO *ME.*

GO INTO THE WORLD AND MAKE DISCIPLES FROM ALL NATIONS, BAPTIZING THEM IN THE NAME OF THE FATHER, THE SON, AND THE HOLY SPIRIT.

YOU WILL RECEIVE *POWER* WHEN THE HOLY SPIRIT COMES, AND YOU WILL BE MY WITNESSES IN JERUSALEM, JUDEA, AND TO THE ENDS OF THE EARTH! YOUR WORK IS ONLY *BEGINNING!*

AND AS HE STOOD THERE BLESSING THEM, HE WAS TAKEN *UP,* BEFORE THEIR EYES...

I AM GOING TO SEND THE ONE MY *FATHER* PROMISED YOU – *THE HOLY SPIRIT.* DO NOT LEAVE JERUSALEM, BUT *WAIT* FOR HIM THERE.

UP INTO *HEAVEN.*

JUST THEN TWO ANGELS APPEARED SAYING, 'MEN OF GALILEE, WHY ARE YOU LOOKING AT THE SKY? JESUS HAS BEEN TAKEN FROM YOU INTO *HEAVEN,* AND IN THE SAME WAY HE WILL *RETURN* TO YOU.'

AND SO THEY RETURNED TO *JERUSALEM.*

AND THERE THEY WAITED...

YOU DO **KNOW** THAT IT IS AGAINST JEWISH LAW FOR ME TO ASSOCIATE WITH GENTILES, OR EVEN **VISIT** THEM?

... NOW I SEE WHAT THE VISION MEANS: **NOTHING** GOD MAKES CLEAN IS UNCLEAN. GOD HAS NO FAVOURITES, BUT WILL ACCEPT **ANYONE** WHO BELIEVES IN HIM.

I KNOW YOU HAVE HEARD WHAT'S BEEN HAPPENING IN JUDEA, AND OF JESUS OF NAZARETH. **EVERYONE** WHO BELIEVES IN HIM RECEIVES FORGIVENESS OF SINS - AND THAT INCLUDES YOU. YOU MUST BE BAPTIZED TOO!

I DO. BUT I WAS PRAYING WHEN AN **ANGEL** TOLD ME TO SEND FOR YOU. ALL THESE PEOPLE ARE DESPERATE TO HEAR WHAT YOU HAVE TO SAY THAT IS SO IMPORTANT.

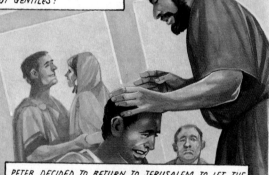

IT WAS JUST AS BEFORE: GOD SENT HIS HOLY SPIRIT, AND PEOPLE SPOKE IN OTHER LANGUAGES. BUT **THIS** TIME, IT WAS NOT **JEWS** WHO RECEIVED GOD'S SPECIAL GIFT, BUT GENTILES!

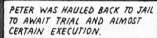

PETER DECIDED TO RETURN TO JERUSALEM TO LET THE JEWISH CHURCH KNOW HIS ASTOUNDING NEWS.

THERE KING HEROD AGRIPPA WAS TRYING TO MAKE HIMSELF POPULAR WITH JEWISH LEADERS BY JOINING THE PERSECUTION.

JAMES, ONE OF THE DISCIPLES, WAS PUT TO THE **SWORD** AT HEROD'S REQUEST. NOW ONLY **TEN** OF THE TWELVE DISCIPLES REMAINED.

PETER WAS HAULED BACK TO JAIL TO AWAIT TRIAL AND ALMOST CERTAIN EXECUTION.

LORD GOD, THERE IS STILL SO MUCH WORK TO BE DONE. SAVE ME FROM THIS, SO I CAN CARRY THE NAME OF **JESUS** TO THE WORLD.

I KNOW **NOTHING** IS IMPOSSIBLE FOR YOU.

HUH? WHAT'S THAT NOISE? IT SOUNDS LIKE...

238

240

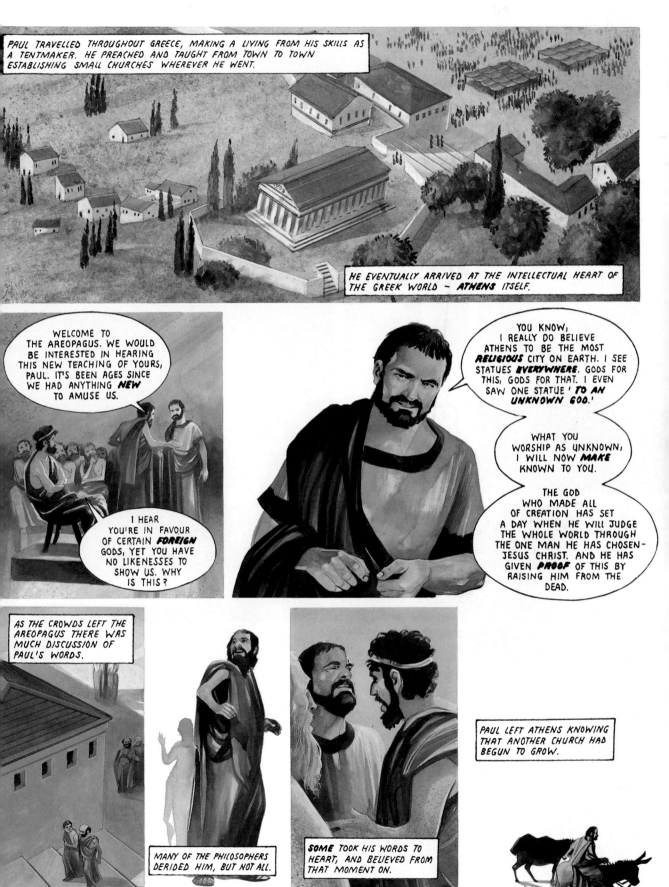

PAUL TRAVELLED THROUGHOUT GREECE, MAKING A LIVING FROM HIS SKILLS AS A TENTMAKER. HE PREACHED AND TAUGHT FROM TOWN TO TOWN ESTABLISHING SMALL CHURCHES WHEREVER HE WENT.

HE EVENTUALLY ARRIVED AT THE INTELLECTUAL HEART OF THE GREEK WORLD — *ATHENS* ITSELF.

WELCOME TO THE AREOPAGUS. WE WOULD BE INTERESTED IN HEARING THIS NEW TEACHING OF YOURS, PAUL. IT'S BEEN AGES SINCE WE HAD ANYTHING *NEW* TO AMUSE US.

I HEAR YOU'RE IN FAVOUR OF CERTAIN *FOREIGN* GODS, YET YOU HAVE NO LIKENESSES TO SHOW US. WHY IS THIS?

YOU KNOW, I REALLY DO BELIEVE ATHENS TO BE THE MOST *RELIGIOUS* CITY ON EARTH. I SEE STATUES *EVERYWHERE*. GODS FOR THIS, GODS FOR THAT. I EVEN SAW ONE STATUE ' *TO AN UNKNOWN GOD.* '

WHAT YOU WORSHIP AS UNKNOWN, I WILL NOW *MAKE* KNOWN TO YOU.

THE GOD WHO MADE ALL OF CREATION HAS SET A DAY WHEN HE WILL JUDGE THE WHOLE WORLD THROUGH THE ONE MAN HE HAS CHOSEN— JESUS CHRIST. AND HE HAS GIVEN *PROOF* OF THIS BY RAISING HIM FROM THE DEAD.

AS THE CROWDS LEFT THE AREOPAGUS THERE WAS MUCH DISCUSSION OF PAUL'S WORDS.

PAUL LEFT ATHENS KNOWING THAT ANOTHER CHURCH HAD BEGUN TO GROW.

MANY OF THE PHILOSOPHERS DERIDED HIM, BUT NOT ALL.

SOME TOOK HIS WORDS TO HEART, AND BELIEVED FROM THAT MOMENT ON.

BUT HIS MISSION WAS FAR FROM OVER. PAUL'S TRAVELS TOOK HIM THROUGH CORINTH TO THE CITY OF EPHESUS.

HE TAUGHT THERE FOR SEVERAL MONTHS, BUILDING UP THE FAITH OF THE NEW CHRISTIANS.

THE NEW FAITH TOOK HOLD. PEOPLE TURNED AWAY FROM WORSHIPPING IDOLS AND DESTROYED THEIR GOLD AND SILVER STATUES. PAUL PREACHED OPENLY AGAINST THE IDOLATRY HE SAW EVERYWHERE.

NONE OF WHICH WENT UNNOTICED BY THE WEALTHY BUSINESSMAN **DEMETRIUS**.

HE WAS A **SILVERSMITH** WHO PROFITED FROM MAKING IDOLS, AND THE CHRISTIANS WERE THREATENING HIS **LIVELIHOOD**.

WITHIN A FEW SHORT WEEKS, EPHESUS WAS A CITY IN **RIOT**.

DEMETRIUS USED HIS CONSIDERABLE INFLUENCE TO STIR FEELINGS AGAINST WHAT HE SAW AS A NEW JEWISH SECT. A CULT WHICH THREATENED THEIR RELIGION, THEIR GODS, THEIR VERY **CULTURE**.

ABOVE ALL, IT WAS BAD FOR **BUSINESS**.

LET ME GO AND **SPEAK** WITH THEM! I MAY BE ABLE TO –

– TO GET YOURSELF **LYNCHED**, PAUL? NO, WE'RE STAYING OUT OF THE WAY UNTIL THIS BLOWS OVER!

TIME TO MOVE ON. THINGS WILL SETTLE DOWN ONCE I'VE GONE.

PAUL TRAVELLED THROUGH MACEDONIA AND GREECE, BUT HIS ULTIMATE GOAL WAS JERUSALEM.

HE HAD RECEIVED WORD OF A **PROPHECY**, THAT THERE HE WOULD BE CAPTURED BY THE JEWS AND HANDED TO THE GENTILES.

ALTHOUGH HE WAS **WILLING** TO DIE FOR HIS FAITH IF NEED BE, HE SET SAIL WITH A HEAVY HEART.

ARE YOU SURE IT'S *LEGAL* TO FLOG ROMAN CITIZENS WITHOUT TRIAL?

NO ONE SAID ANYTHING ABOUT YOU BEING A *CITIZEN.*

HOW DID YOU GAIN CITIZENSHIP? I HAD TO PAY *DEARLY* FOR MINE.

I WAS *BORN* A CITIZEN. AND I KNOW THE LAW WELL ENOUGH TO KNOW THAT YOU CAN'T FLOG A CITIZEN WITHOUT TRIAL.

TO PREVENT HIM BEING TORN APART BY THE MOB, THE COMMANDER OF THE GARRISON HAD HIM PLACED IN PROTECTIVE CUSTODY. BUT GOD HAD SPOKEN TO PAUL, SAYING, 'JUST AS YOU WERE MY WITNESS IN JERUSALEM, SO WILL YOU BE IN *ROME.'*

IT SEEMED PAUL WAS TO SPEND THE REST OF HIS LIFE AS A *PRISONER.*

BUT A SMALL GROUP OF JEWS TOOK A SOLEMN VOW NOT TO EAT OR DRINK UNTIL PAUL WAS DEAD.

THEY ASKED THE JEWISH COUNCIL TO SEND FOR PAUL.

ONCE HE'S LEFT THE PALACE, WE'LL KILL HIM.

THEIR PLOT WAS OVERHEARD BY PAUL'S NEPHEW. WHEN THE ROMAN COMMANDER GOT TO HEAR OF IT HE DECIDED TO GET PAUL OUT OF JERUSALEM AT ONCE.

IN THE DEAD OF NIGHT PAUL WAS ESCORTED FROM THE FORT TO TRAVEL TO THE ROMAN HEADQUARTERS AT CAESAREA.

PAUL WAS CALLED TO DEFEND HIMSELF BEFORE THE ROMAN GOVERNOR, BUT HIS CASE WAS NEVER SETTLED. HE WAS RUNNING OUT OF PATIENCE.

TAKE DOWN THIS MESSAGE.

I APPEAL TO CAESAR. I AM A ROMAN CITIZEN AND I WISH TO EXERCISE MY RIGHT TO HAVE MY CASE HEARD IN ROME BY THE EMPEROR HIMSELF.

AND SO, JUST AS HAD BEEN PROPHESIED, PAUL SET SAIL FOR THE VERY HEART OF THE WORLD, AND OF THE GREATEST EMPIRE EVER SEEN.

ROME.

PAUL WAS GREEK-EDUCATED, JEWISH BY BIRTH, AND A ROMAN CITIZEN INTO THE BARGAIN. THERE WAS NO ONE AS QUALIFIED TO CARRY GOD'S MESSAGE THROUGHOUT THE ROMAN WORLD.

FROM MOUTH TO MOUTH, HEART TO HEART, THE NAME OF JESUS SPREAD ALONG THE ARROW-STRAIGHT ROADS OF THE EMPIRE.

INDEED, IT WAS **BECAUSE** OF THE CLOSELY KNIT EMPIRE THAT THE MESSAGE SPREAD SO FAST.

BUT THE ROMANS WERE AS CRUEL AS THEY WERE CIVILIZED, THEIR CREATIVE MINDS TURNING TO TORTURE AS READILY AS TO ENGINEERING OR PHILOSOPHY.

THE EMPEROR **NERO**, SEEKING SCAPEGOATS FOR THE GREAT FIRE OF ROME, HURLED THE BLAME SQUARELY AT THE FEET OF THE CHRISTIANS.

MANY MET THEIR DEATHS IN THE ARENA, SOME EATEN ALIVE BY WILD ANIMALS, SOME SLAUGHTERED BY GLADIATORS.

THE ROMANS TOOK SUCH DELIGHT IN WATCHING AGONIZING, HUMILIATING DEATHS THAT BEING THROWN TO THE LIONS WAS FAR FROM THE **WORST** DEATH POSSIBLE.

OF THE FINAL END OF THE DISCIPLES, NO **OFFICIAL** RECORDS SURVIVE THOSE DARK DAYS. SOME LEGENDS SAY THAT THOMAS MADE IT AS FAR AS **INDIA**, AND PAUL TO **SPAIN**, ONLY TO BE EVENTUALLY BEHEADED BY THE ROMANS.

PETER WAS ALSO CAPTURED. DYING ON A ROMAN CROSS, HIS LAST REQUEST WAS THAT HE BE CRUCIFIED UPSIDE DOWN, CONSIDERING HIMSELF **UNWORTHY** OF EVEN THE SAME **DEATH** AS HIS BELOVED JESUS.

IN 70AD, SOME JEWS — NOT BELIEVING THE MESSIAH HAD BEEN AND GONE — GREW TIRED OF WAITING AND ROSE UP IN ARMS AGAINST THE ROMAN OCCUPIERS.

HALF-TRAINED ZEALOTS WERE NO THREAT TO THE MOST DISCIPLINED, WELL-TRAINED FIGHTING MEN THE WORLD HAD SEEN. THE BATTLE QUICKLY BECAME A **MASSACRE**.

IN THE ENSUING CHAOS, THE TEMPLE IN JERUSALEM WAS DESTROYED, AS HAD BEEN PREDICTED. IT REMAINS A RUIN TO THIS DAY.

OF THE MEN WHO HAD KNOWN JESUS IN HIS TIME ON EARTH, **ONE** STILL LIVED — A **PRISONER** IN THE WORK CAMP ON THE ISLAND OF **PATMOS**.

HIS NAME WAS **JOHN**. AND IT IS FROM HIM THAT THE LAST STORY OF THEM ALL COMES. FOR JUST AS ADAM SAW THE WORLD WHEN IT WAS NEW, SO GOD ALLOWED JOHN TO SEE IT AT ITS **END**.

IT WAS EARLY IN THE MORNING. I, JOHN, THE LAST OF THE DISCIPLES WHO SAW GOD WALK ON EARTH, STOOD AT THE EDGE OF THE SEA, AND FELT THE DESPAIR WELL UP IN ME.

THERE ON PATMOS, BETWEEN THE LAND AND SKY, I STOOD AND WEPT, NOT KNOWING WHY OUR GOD HAD NOT YET RETURNED TO US.

SURELY IF HE WERE EVER TO RETURN IT WOULD BE **NOW**, I THOUGHT. YET HE HAD NOT.

HOW LONG WOULD WE HAVE TO WAIT? MONTHS? YEARS? CENTURIES? **MILLENNIA**?

BUT THEN I **HEARD** IT... A **VOICE**.

A VOICE BEHIND ME, AS LOUD AS **TRUMPETS**! AS LOUD AS **THUNDER**!

AND THE VOICE SAID:

'WRITE DOWN ALL YOU SEE AND SEND IT TO THE CHURCHES. DO NOT BE AFRAID! I AM THE **FIRST**, AND THE **LAST**. I WAS DEAD, BUT NOW I AM ALIVE **FOR EVER**!'

I SAW A GREAT **SCROLL**, FASTENED WITH SEVEN SEALS, BUT THERE WAS NO ONE **WORTHY** ENOUGH TO BREAK THEM, EXCEPT ONE.

I SAW THE ONE PERSON WHO HAD WON THE RIGHT — THE SON OF DAVID. HE SEEMED TO ME TO BE AS POWERFUL AS A **LION** ONE MOMENT, AND YET AS MEEK AS A **LAMB** THE NEXT.

HE BROKE THE FIRST FOUR SEALS, ONE BY ONE, AND OUT RODE FOUR TERRIFYING **HORSEMEN**. THERE WOULD BE NONE ON EARTH WHO COULD **STOP** THEM...

THE FIRST RODE A HORSE AS WHITE AS **DISEASE**, AS COLD AS **DESPAIR**. HE WENT OUT TO CONQUER THE WORLD IN THE NAME OF GOD'S **ENEMIES**.

THE SECOND WAS AS RED AS **BLOODSHED**, AS RED AS **ANGER**. HE HELD A TERRIBLE SWORD, AND BROUGHT WAR AND VIOLENCE TO ALL THE EARTH.

THE THIRD HORSE WAS AS BLACK AS **MURDER**, AS DARK AS **HUNGER**. THE RIDER HELD HIGH A PAIR OF SCALES, AND SPREAD STARVATION AND FAMINE WHEREVER HE WENT.

AND AS FOR THE FOURTH RIDER... THE FOURTH WAS **DEATH**, AND WHERE THE OTHER THREE WENT, HE FOLLOWED IN THEIR WAKE.

AND THEN THE FIFTH SEAL BROKE, AND I HEARD THE VOICES OF ALL THOSE WHO HAD BEEN MURDERED BECAUSE THEY SPOKE THE TRUTH ABOUT GOD.

WITH ONE VOICE THEY CRIED OUT TO GOD: 'HOW LONG BEFORE OUR DEATHS ARE AVENGED?'

AS THE SIXTH SEAL BROKE, THE SUN BECAME BLACK.

THE MOON TURNED BLOOD-RED AND THE STARS FELL FROM THE SKY.

MASSIVE EARTHQUAKES SHOOK EVERY MOUNTAIN AND ISLAND FROM ITS PLACE.

ALL PEOPLE, FROM THE HIGHEST TO THE LOWEST, RAN TO HIDE FROM THE AWESOME WRATH OF GOD.

I SAW FOUR ANGELS STANDING AT THE FOUR CORNERS OF THE WORLD, HOLDING BACK THE FOUR WINDS.

AND THERE WAS A VAST CROWD OF PEOPLE, SO MANY THAT I COULD NOT COUNT THEM.

FROM EVERY COUNTRY, EVERY STATE, CITY, TRIBE AND NATION, THEY STOOD IN FRONT OF THE LAMB OF GOD, SHOUTING 'SALVATION BELONGS TO OUR GOD! AND IT COMES FROM THE LAMB OF GOD!'

AND THEN THE SEVENTH SEAL WAS OPENED.

THERE STOOD BEFORE ME A WOMAN IN LABOUR, WHO CRIED OUT, FOR SHE WAS SOON TO GIVE BIRTH.

AND THEN I SAW IT.

THE DRAGON. THE SEVEN-HEADED, HORNED SERPENT, SATAN, IN ITS TRUE FORM. IT TRIED TO EAT THE CHILD AS IT WAS BORN, BUT THE CHILD WAS RESCUED AND TAKEN TO GOD.

AND THERE WAS WAR IN HEAVEN.

THE ARCHANGEL MICHAEL AND HIS ANGELS ATTACKED THE SERPENT, WHO FOUGHT BACK WITH HIS ANGELS.

AND I SAW **BABYLON**, AND I WATCHED IT BURN. AND UNDERSTOOD WHY IT WAS THAT THE DRAGON HAD SEVEN HEADS, FOR THE CITY THAT I WATCHED BURNING WAS THE HEART OF THE EVIL **EMPIRE**, AND ALSO SAT ON SEVEN **HILLS**.

AND THEN... OH! **HEAVEN** OPENED, AND I **SAW** HIM!! I SAW HIM AGAIN WITH MY OWN **EYES**!

IT WAS THE **LORD**, AND HE CAME RIDING A WHITE HORSE, WITH ALL THE ARMIES OF HEAVEN BEHIND HIM, BRINGING **JUSTICE** FOR ALL.

THEN I SAW MICHAEL, THE ARCHANGEL, COMING DOWN FROM HEAVEN HOLDING IN HIS HAND THE KEY TO HELL AND CARRYING A GREAT CHAIN.

THE DEVIL WAS BOUND AND THROWN INTO A BOTTOMLESS PIT, AND IT WAS LOCKED AND SEALED SO THAT HE MIGHT DECEIVE NO MORE.

THEN I LOOKED AGAIN AND SAW EVERYONE WHO HAD EVER LIVED, STANDING BEFORE THE LORD. THE HISTORIES OF THEIR LIVES WERE READ, AND THEY WERE JUDGED ON HOW THEY HAD LIVED; THE EVIL DESTROYED, THE GOOD SAVED.

AND WHEN THEY HAD BEEN JUDGED **DEATH ITSELF** WAS DESTROYED TOO.

256

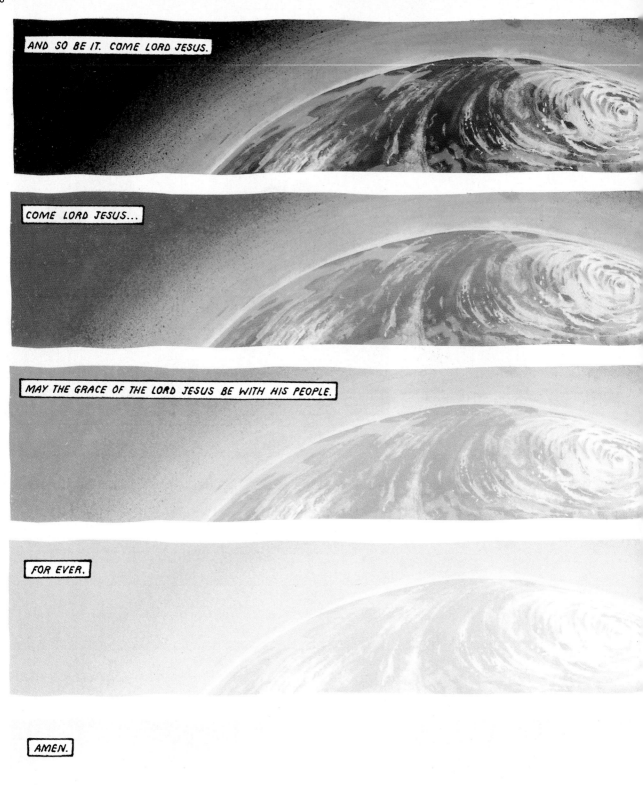